PUSHMATAHA

PUSHMATAHA

A Choctaw Leader and His People

Gideon Lincecum

With an Introduction by Greg O'Brien

The University of Alabama Press

Tuscaloosa

Copyright © 2004
The University of Alabama Press
Tuscaloosa, Alabama 35487-0380
All rights reserved
Manufactured in the United States of America

Typeface: Galliard

∞
The paper on which this book is printed meets the minimum requirements of
American National Standard for Information Science–Permanence of Paper for
Printed Library Materials, ANSI Z39.48-1984.

Library of Congress Cataloging-in-Publication Data

Lincecum, Gideon, 1793–1874.
 Pushmataha : a Choctaw leader and his people / Gideon Lincecum ; with an
introduction by Greg O'Brien.
  p. cm.
 Includes bibliographical references and index.
 ISBN 0-8173-5115-9 (pbk. : alk. paper)
 1. Pushmataha, ca. 1764–1824 2. Choctaw Indians—Kings and rulers—
Biography. 3. Choctaw Indians—History. 4. Choctaw Indians—Social life
and customs. 5. Mounds—Mississippi. 6. Mississippi—Antiquities. I. Title.
E99.C8P89 2004
976.004'97387—dc22

                                             2003027607

  ISBN 978-0-8173-5115-1   (pbk. : alk. paper)
  ISBN 978-0-8173-8469-2   (electronic)

CONTENTS

Introduction *vii*
        Greg O'Brien

Choctaw Traditions about their Settlement in Mississippi and the
Origin of their Mounds *1*
        Gideon Lincecum

Life of Apushimataha *26*
        Gideon Lincecum

INTRODUCTION

Greg O'Brien

GIDEON LINCECUM (1793–1874) received little formal educa-tion, but he was a voracious reader and self-taught physician, naturalist, ethnologist, folklorist, and philosopher. He listened to and observed carefully people and the natural environment; prac-ticed medicine throughout his life; collected plant and animal speci-mens; corresponded with notable naturalists such as Charles Dar-win (sending him forty-eight samples of Texas ants with detailed commentaries); dabbled in geology; recorded weather observations; tracked drought cycles; was a devoted freethinker and atheist; learned to write and speak the Choctaw language; and preserved Choctaw knowledge about medicinal plants, the afterlife, the tribe's origins, and its history. In his lifetime, he contributed plant and animal col-lections to the Philadelphia Academy of Science and the Smith-sonian Institution and wrote articles for the *American Naturalist,* the *American Sportsman,* the *Proceedings of the Academy of Natural Sciences,* the *Journal of the Linnaean Society,* the *Texas Almanac,* and for various newspapers, as well as a detailed account of his life and an unpublished history of the Choctaw people.[1] After his death, Lincecum's daughter, Sallie Doran, inherited his remaining papers and collections. Most of them eventually ended up in the archives of the University of Texas, where they still reside and are available for study.[2] Doran also released three of Lincecum's writings, or ex-cerpts of his writings, for publication to the Mississippi Historical Society in the early twentieth century, two of which are republished here.[3]

In 1818 the Lincecum family—including twenty-five-year-old Gideon, his wife, Sarah, their two small children, his parents,

Hezekiah and Sally, various siblings, and several African American slaves—joined scores of other new American settlers along the Tombigbee River in the new state of Mississippi. They initially settled near present-day Columbus, Mississippi, and then in 1820 along the route of what became the federal road, sometimes called "Jackson's military road," that connected New Orleans, Louisiana, with Nashville, Tennessee, via Columbus. The Lincecums sought a new start after moving repeatedly in the preceding years between South Carolina, Georgia, and the Alabama Territory. The seemingly boundless natural resources of the Tombigbee River area and the remoteness of their new settlement appealed mightily to Lincecum; he and his family marveled at the large numbers of deer, bear, turkeys, ducks, and fish. "Suffice it to say," Lincecum wrote, "we were all greatly pleased, and supplied our table with a superabundance of fish, fowl, and venison, and occasionally a glorious fleece of bear meat."[4] The Lincecums relished the frontier setting of the upper Tombigbee region and, though they moved around with some regularity, making Cotton Gin Port their home from 1825 to 1833, they lived in the region until 1848, when they moved further west to Texas.

Two factors make Gideon Lincecum's thirty-year stay in Mississippi of great value to us today. First, he possessed a tremendous sense of inquisitiveness about the natural and human environment surrounding him, preserving his observations in letters, specimen collections, histories, and autobiographical essays. There exist few records that describe as well as Lincecum's what life was like for pioneering American families in early-nineteenth-century Mississippi and the Old Southwest. Lincecum and his family experienced all of the joys and hardships of other settlers. Lincecum forged friendships with many of the wealthiest and most powerful men of the Tombigbee River region, including John Pitchlynn, a white man who had been raised among and resided in the Choctaw Nation with a Choctaw wife and several children and who happened to be a second cousin of Lincecum's mother, Sally Hickman Lincecum. Pitchlynn was also the principal interpreter for the Choctaws whenever they met with American diplomats, and he had grown very wealthy by raising cattle, growing cotton, and owning slaves. Lincecum started a trading business with one of Pitchlynn's sons, named John, Jr.[5] Lincecum impressed his new neighbors with his intellect, honesty, humility, and sobriety, and they responded throughout his three decades in Mississippi with loans, business partnerships, and advice. He needed, though almost never asked for, help on occasion as his wide-ranging aptitude led him to try several different means of employment. Though he desired financial stability, Lincecum quit one occupation after another if he grew bored, found the work distasteful, or his health required it. While living in Mississippi, Lincecum logged trees and sold lumber; traded commodities to Indians for furs and other items; was the first chief justice, chairman of the school commissioners, and superintendent of the new male and female academies in Monroe County in eastern Mississippi; turned down an offer to run for the state legislature; and served as a doctor in an unofficial capacity before establishing himself as a full-time doctor in the Cotton Gin Port area in 1830.[6]

Lincecum's family grew from two children to nine while in Mississippi, and their education became a matter of particular concern. Although he had received little formal education and was self-taught, Gideon justifiably regarded himself as intellectually enlightened and wanted the same or better for his children. Subsequent to earning some money practicing medicine, Lincecum established his wife in Columbus in order to send their six school-age children to the seminaries there. After six months he journeyed down from Cotton Gin Port to see them and discover the state of their learning at "the highly lauded seminary." Unfortunately, in Lincecum's view, the schools taught his children nothing but Bible stories, rather than history, geography, or other practical knowledge. "I was overwhelmed with disappointment," he remembered. "I felt that the whole world was a sham. My children after six months' constant attendance on that highly praised institution could answer no question of use." Bitter at the school's "infernal foolishness," Lincecum recollected that "I was deeply wounded in my feelings and expectations and I decided at once to take them away from the hypocritical place." Promptly, the entire family returned to Cotton Gin Port.

The subject of education does not resurface in Lincecum's *Autobiography*, and it is supposed that he relied on a version of what today is called "home schooling" to educate his children.[7] Lincecum's formidable list of accomplishments masks some of the hardship he and his family endured while in Mississippi. In addition to his fickleness over establishing a career, Lincecum frequently took ill for extended periods of time, with symptoms that suggest some sort of heart ailment. His bouts of sickness left him without a means to procure an income for months at a time and placed great stress on his family members to provide for themselves. The threat of debilitating disease remained a constant for everyone in early Mississippi; Lincecum stated that "one or more of his family was sick all the time," including their slaves.[8] Epidemics of cholera, dysentery (sometimes called the "bloody flux"), and various "fevers" afflicted everyone in the region around this time. Lincecum became convinced that the traditional medicine of his day, consisting of "bleeding" the patient and prescribing assorted emetics and "poisons," did more harm than good. "I felt tired of killing people," he griped, "and concluded to quit the man-killing practice and try to procure a living by some other method."[9] Moreover, Lincecum complained that medical journals written by northerners failed to adequately address the environmental and medical conditions of the South. Increasingly disillusioned with the state of learning in Euro-American society, he happened upon an ingenious solution to better treat southern ailments: "the plan I had conceived was to visit an Indian doctor of great reputation, who resided in the Six Towns, Choctaw Nation, and try to get him to show me what he knew of medicine and disease." For six weeks in the early 1830s, Lincecum absorbed the teachings of Eliccha Chito, who welcomed the chance to preserve his knowledge in written form for future generations. Lincecum had long since learned to speak and write Choctaw and wrote a large manuscript in Choctaw based on what Eliccha Chito told him about plant-based remedies. From that point forward, Lincecum utilized herbal treatments in his medical practice. Although this manuscript has apparently been lost and was not widely disseminated, his new-found information was shared with others, patients and doctors alike, and is a remarkable example of the blending of cultural traditions that occurred throughout the South as Indians, Euro-Americans, and Africans learned from one another.[10]

As his visit with the Choctaw healer suggests, Lincecum's second major contribution deriving from his years in Mississippi is information on the area's indigenous inhabitants. He and his family had moved next door to two of the most significant American Indian populations in the Southeast, the Choctaws and the Chickasaws, and Lincecum soon established friendly relationships with many of his Indian neighbors, eventually learning their language and many of their traditions. Lincecum has been rightly criticized for his sometimes-florid prose and propensity to exaggerate certain aspects of Choctaw culture or dialogue.[11] Nevertheless, it is obvious from his writings that he valued Indian people as equal and admirable human beings worthy of being listened to and consulted. He tended to blame outside influences, such as alcohol, rather than anything inherent to Indian cultures for the problems Indians experienced in the nineteenth century, writing caustically at one point that "if there could be born an honest, liberty-loving leader who would take things in hand, concentrate the Indian forces, capture all the praying white races and their allies, the mixed-blood cut throats, and chop off their damn heads, there would remain the most innocent, law-abiding people on earth—the pure Indian."[12] More myth than reality, the "pure Indian" nonetheless played a large role in Lincecum's life and thoughts.

Lincecum sympathized with the antiremoval position when the clamor for Indian relocation west of the Mississippi River became government policy, and he expectedly criticized the role of Christian missionaries among the Indians. The Mississippi legislature passed a law extending state jurisdiction over all Indian territory within its boundaries in 1829, thus forcing the federal government and President Andrew Jackson to support the effort with the federal Indian Removal Act of 1830, laying the legal groundwork for the forced banishment of eastern Indians to the West.[13] Amid the backdrop of this political maneuvering, and seeking a way to make some money after a disabling illness, Lincecum organized a team of Choctaw stickball players to tour the United States. Through his friend and relative John Pitchlynn, Lincecum contacted a Choctaw man named Fulahooma, who arranged for Choctaw volunteers to meet Lincecum and join the ball-playing excursion. Fulahooma and Lincecum intended to take forty players on the tour but more than four hundred appeared at the assembly with Lincecum. They "were mad with their chiefs," explained Fulahooma, and told Lincecum "that their head men had sold their homes and made them very poor; that they were willing to travel with [him] any length of time, just for their victuals and clothes."[14] Lincecum and Fulahooma conducted a rigged lottery with forty prechosen names for the team, but the other players never suspected the deception. For eight months in 1829–30 the team toured the United States yet only made enough money to pay for their immediate supplies. Still, Lincecum returned to Mississippi refreshed and healthier and his Choctaw team appreciated his efforts to secure some income for them, dubbing him "Hogipeh cheto," which Lincecum translated as "Big leader."[15] During his contact with the Choctaws, they called him by two other names as well: "Shappo Tohoba" (White Hat), because he wore a white hat when he began trading with the Choctaws soon after arriving in Mississippi, and "Anumpatashula ebisya" (Interpreter's nephew), for his relationship with John Pitchlynn.[16]

In addition to Lincecum's interest in obtaining medical knowledge from the Choctaws and transacting business with them, he also developed a preoccupation with their history and traditions. He visited "the oldest man in the world, a man that knew everything" named Chahta Immataha several times between 1823 and 1825 to learn about Choctaw history and the origins of their mounds. Chahta Immataha, who claimed "I am, and I regret that it is true, the only man left who can repeat correctly the Shukhah-anumpula [literally, 'hog talk,' the Choctaw name for their traditional history]," gave Lincecum a long version of the Choctaw past, including the detailed "Choctaw Traditions About Their Settlement in Mississippi and the Origin of Their Mounds," reprinted in this volume.[17] It is clear that Lincecum learned a version of Choctaw history that closely mirrors other recorded versions from the eighteenth and early nineteenth centuries, though the amount of embellishment by Lincecum is harder to gauge. It is also likely that Chahta Immataha's version of the Choctaw migration to Mississippi is one of several different, equally valid accounts of Choctaw origins in Mississippi that reflect the diverse ethnic groups of the Choctaw confederacy. There existed among the Choctaws three principal geographic and political divisions that also maintained separate ethnic identities—the western (Okla Falaya), eastern (Okla Tannap), and Six Towns (Okla Hannali) divisions. The western division villages were scattered around the upper Pearl River watershed, and the eastern division towns were located around the upper Chickasawhay River and Tombigbee River watersheds. The Six Towns were distributed along the upper Leaf River and mid-Chickasawhay River watersheds.[18] It is also plausible that Chahta Immataha purposely left out some details about Choctaw traditions, too sacred for non-Choctaw ears. Despite these caveats, Chahta Immataha's stories, as retold by Lincecum, deserve close attention. He has much to say about why the Choctaws migrated to central Mississippi; when they did so; why they erected their sacred Nanih Waya mound and other earthen structures (including the role of women in constructing certain types of mounds); how they formed new towns; the role of various types of chiefs and religious specialists in leading Choctaw society; burial customs; and Choctaw spirituality. Lincecum excavated a number of mounds soon after talking with Chahta Immataha and verified some of the information he was given. Contemporary archaeologists and other scholars should also use accounts like the one preserved by Lincecum to verify their interpretations of Mississippi Indian cultures.[19]

When the state and federal government removal policies went into effect against the Choctaws in 1831 and the first groups of Choctaws began the journey to Indian Territory (present-day Oklahoma), Lincecum felt real sadness at the fate of his Indian friends. Although he remained ethnocentric in believing the Choctaws to be "innocent" and "unsophisticated," despite all he had learned from them, his memories of a group of removed Choctaws passing his house on a cold night in November 1831 on their "trail of tears" evoked genuine emotion:

> I remember now, though the time has long passed, with feelings of unfeigned gratitude the many kindnesses bestowed on me and my little family in 1818 and 1819 when we were in their neighborhood, before the country began to fill up with other white people. . . . We met often, hunted together, fished together, swam together, and they were positively and I have no hesitation in declaring it here, the most truthful, most reliable and best people I have ever dealt with. While we resided in their country my wife had a very severe spell of fever that confined her to bed for several weeks . . . kind hearted Chahta women would come often, bringing with them their nicely prepared *tampulo* water for her to drink, and remaining by the sick bed for hours at a time. . . . The time is long gone, and I may never have the pleasure of meeting with any of that most excellent race of people. But so long as the life pendulum swings in this old time-shattered bosom, I shall remember their many kindnesses to me and mine, with sentiments of kindest affection and deepest gratitude.[20]

The republication of Lincecum's articles on the Choctaw chief Pushmataha and on Choctaw beliefs about their origins and the creation of their mounds brings back into print valuable and difficult-to-find resources on Choctaw history and culture. Lincecum's essay about Pushmataha is the closest to a firsthand account of that chief's life that we are ever likely to get. Pushmataha, "the great man of the [Choctaw] nation and of the age" according to Lincecum, stayed at Lincecum's house several times, and Lincecum also interviewed other Choctaws about the chief's past.[21] Some of Pushmataha's life as a chief and diplomat can be traced through government records dating from the War of 1812, the papers of Andrew Jackson, and records of early-nineteenth-century treaty negotiations between the Choctaws and the United States. As an adult, Pushmataha resided in the Six Towns division (Okla Hannali) of the Choctaw confederacy (the same division where the medicine man Eliccha Chito lived), and it was that division he represented in diplomatic meetings. Sometime around 1800, Pushmataha became a leading chief and began playing a major role in negotiations with other peoples, especially the Americans. He quickly developed a well-deserved reputation for his eloquent speaking abilities, and he was able to persuade both Choctaws and Americans with his sharp logic and lyrical speaking style. The first formal treaty with the United States that he took part in was the Fort Confederation meeting in 1802. From that point onward, Pushmataha played an important role in all dealings between the Choctaws and the United States. When the Red Stick Creek Indians attacked Fort Mims in August 1813, for example, Pushmataha organized a Choctaw fighting force that assisted Andrew Jackson in defeating the Red Sticks. Pushmataha also participated in the Treaty of Doak's Stand with the United States in 1820 that called for Choctaw removal to lands west of the Mississippi River. He informed his former ally Andrew Jackson that the lands in the west (present-day Arkansas) were too poor to support agriculture and hunting and that white settlers already lived there. Pushmataha tried to get a promise from Jackson to evict the white settlers, but this issue was never settled and it brought Pushmataha and other Choctaw chiefs to Washington, D.C., in 1824. During the 1824 negotiations, Pushmataha became sick and died and was buried with full military honors in the Congressional Cemetery in Washington, D.C.

Pushmataha's early life before becoming a principal chief, however, is shrouded in secrecy, and Lincecum fills in some of these gaps as no other source can. Pushmataha's war exploits as a young man, especially in killing Native enemies of the Choctaws west of the Mississippi River, became famous throughout the lower Mississippi Valley. Although the details of Pushmataha's war exploits as portrayed by Lincecum stretch believability, there is little doubt that Pushmataha achieved greatness as a warrior. All of these military actions earned the respect of other Choctaws, and several chiefs and spiritual leaders bestowed the title that we know him by today: Pushmataha, or rather "Apushamatahahubi," means "a messenger of death; literally one whose rifle, tomahawk, or bow is alike fatal in war or hunting."[22] Americans of the early nineteenth century simplified his name to Pushmataha or even "Push." A mystery surrounding Pushmataha is the identity of his parents. They may have been killed by the Creeks or other enemies of the Choctaws when he was young, as Lincecum reported. Most likely they were commoners because Pushmataha expressed uneasiness about his kin ties throughout his life. There existed leading or elite families among the Choctaws, and formal leadership positions were often passed down through the generations of these families. Pushmataha had no such kinship connections, but his exceptional record of achievement based upon the traditional measures of success in war and mastery of spiritual powers meant that he should assume a chiefly position. Accordingly, men like Pushmataha became diplomats and represented their people in meetings with Europeans, Americans, and other Indians.[23]

Although Lincecum's two articles republished in this book should not be considered the final word on Choctaw mounds, history, or the life of Pushmataha, they are indispensable sources of information on all of those topics. Lincecum understood the Choctaw language and interacted with Choctaw people to an extent unmatched by most subsequent non-Choctaw students of Choctaw culture and history. His command of written Choctaw and English impresses us still and compels our attention.

Notes

1. This information is gleaned from numerous sources, including Lois Wood Burkhalter, *Gideon Lincecum, 1793–1874: A Biography* (Austin: University of Texas Press, 1965); *Adventures of a Frontier Naturalist: The Life and Times of Dr. Gideon Lincecum* (College Station: Texas A&M University Press, 1994); William C. Davis, *A Way through the Wilderness: The Natchez Trace and the Civilization of the Southern Frontier* (Baton Rouge: Louisiana State University Press, 1995); and *Science on the Texas Frontier: Observations of Dr. Gideon Lincecum* (College Station: Texas A&M University Press, 1997). Lincecum's unpublished "Traditional History of the Chahta People," in the University of Texas at Austin, Center for American History archives, was examined by Cheri Lynn Wolfe in her dissertation "The 'Traditional History of the Chahta People': An Analysis of Gideon Lincecum's 19th Century Narrative" (PhD diss., University of Texas at Austin, 1993).

2. See the University of Texas at Austin, Center for American History, "A Guide to the Gideon Lincecum Collection, 1821–1933," http://www.lib.utexas.edu/taro/utcah/00119/cah-00119.html.

3. See "Autobiography of Gideon Lincecum," *Publications of the Mississippi Historical Society* 8 (1905): 443–519; Gideon Lincecum, "Choctaw Traditions About Their Settlement in Mississippi and the Origin of Their Mounds," *Publications of the Mississippi Historical Society* 8 (1904): 521–42; and Gideon Lincecum, "Life of Apushimataha," *Publications of the Mississippi Historical Society* 9 (1906): 415–85.

4. "Autobiography of Gideon Lincecum," 470.

5. On the Pitchlynn family see W. David Baird, *Peter Pitchlynn: Chief of the Choctaws* (Norman: University of Oklahoma Press, 1972).

6. This outline of Lincecum's various professional activities while in Mississippi is taken from "Autobiography of Gideon Lincecum." See also Davis, *A Way through the Wilderness*, 238.

7. "Autobiography of Gideon Lincecum," 491–93.

8. Ibid., 476.

9. Ibid., 493.

10. Ibid., 494–97. See also Burkhalter, *Gideon Lincecum*, 28; T. N. Campbell, "Medicinal Plants Used by Choctaw, Chickasaw, and Creek Indians in the Early Nineteenth Century," *Journal of the Washington Academy of Sciences* 41 (1951): 285–90; and Peter Wood, "'You Would Have Made Such a Good Indian': Passages from the Autobiography of Gideon Lincecum," *Southern Exposure* 13 (1985): 62–66.

11. See John R. Swanton, *Source Material for the Social and Ceremonial Life of the Choctaw Indians* (1931; reprint, Tuscaloosa: University of Alabama Press, 2001), 27.

12. Quoted in Burkhalter, *Gideon Lincecum*, 24.

13. See James Taylor Carson, "State Rights and Indian Removal in Mississippi, 1817–1835," *Journal of Mississippi History* 57 (1995): 25–41.

14. Quotations from "Autobiography of Gideon Lincecum," 484.

15. Ibid., 483–85. See also Burkhalter, *Gideon Lincecum*, 29–30; Wood, "'You Would Have Made Such a Good Indian,'" 62–66; and Davis, *A Way through the Wilderness*, 124.

16. "Autobiography of Gideon Lincecum," 476.

17. Chahta Immataha's quotations are from *Adventures of a Frontier Naturalist*, 97.

18. On the Choctaw divisions, see Patricia Galloway, *Choctaw Genesis, 1500–1700* (Lincoln: University of Nebraska Press, 1995), 140–43; and Greg O'Brien, *Choctaws in a Revolutionary Age, 1750–1830* (Lincoln: University of Nebraska Press, 2002), 12–19.

19. One scholar who used Chahta Immataha's narrative held by the University of Texas at Austin, Center for American History archives is T. N. Campbell, in "The Choctaw Afterworld," *Journal of American Folklore* 72 (1959): 146–54.

20. Quoted in Burkhalter, *Gideon Lincecum,* 30; *Adventures of a Frontier Naturalist,* 75–76; and Lincecum, "Life of Apushimataha," 415–17.

21. Quotation from Lincecum, "Life of Apushimataha," 421.

22. Swanton, *Source Material,* 121.

23. O'Brien, *Choctaws in a Revolutionary Age,* 28–32.

PUSHMATAHA

CHOCTAW TRADITIONS ABOUT THEIR SETTLEMENT IN MISSISSIPPI AND THE ORIGIN OF THEIR MOUNDS

Gideon Lincecum

The chief halted the advance body of Choctaws on a little river to wait until scouts could be sent forward to explore the region of country round about; and to give time for the aged and feeble and those who were overloaded to come up. Many of the families were loaded with so many of the bones of their deceased relatives that they could carry nothing else, and they got along very slowly. At this stage of their long journey, there were a greater number of skeletons being packed along by the people, than there were of the living. The smallest families were heaviest loaded; and such were their adoration and affections for these dry bones, that before they could consent to leave them on the way, they would, having more bones than they could pack at one load, carry forward a part of them half a day's journey, and returning for the remainder, bring them up the next day. By this double traveling over the route, they were soon left a great distance in the rear. They would have preferred to die and rot with these bones in the wilderness, sooner than leave them behind.

The minko looked upon the notions of the people in regard to the extraordinary and overwhelming burthen of bones as a great evil; and he cast in his mind for some plausible excuse to rid the people of a burthen that was as useless as it was oppressive to them. And now the scouts had returned, and the reports they made of quite an extensive excursion were very favorable and encouraging. They stated that everywhere, and in all directions, they found game of all sorts, fish and fowl and fruits in abundance; tall trees and running brooks; altogether they looked upon it as the most desirable and plentiful region they had found during their pilgrimage. They also stated, that the most convenient place they had found, for a winter encampment, lay in a southeasterly direction at the junction of three large creeks, which coming together at the same point, formed an immense lowland, and a considerable river. In the fork of the first and the middle creeks lay an extensive range of dry, good lands, covered with tall trees of various kinds, grapes, nuts, and acorns; and rivulets (bok ushi) of running water. For the multitude, it was distant eight or ten days' travel, and the route would be less and less difficult to that place.

At the rising of the sun on the ensuing morning, the leader's pole was observed to be inclining to the southeast, and the people were moving off quite early. The nights were becoming cooler, and they desired to have time to prepare shelter before the winter rains should commence. The chief, with the Isht Ahullo, who carried the sacred pole, went in front, and being good walkers, they traveled rapidly until they came to the place which had been designated. Great numbers of the stronger and more athletic people came up the same day.

Early on the next morning the chief went to observe the leader's pole, which, at the moment of sunrise, danced and punched itself deeper into the ground; and after some time settled in a perpendicular position, without having nodded or bowed in any direction. Seeing which the chief said, "It is well. We have arrived at our winter encampment." He gave instructions to the tool carriers to lay off the encampment for the iksas and mark on the posts their appropriate symbols. He ordered them to allow sufficient space for the iksas, having particular regard to the watering places.

It was several days before the people had all reached the encampment. Those who were packing the double loads of bones came in several days later, and they complained of being greatly fatigued. They mourned and said, "The bad spirit has killed our kindred; to pack their bones any further will kill us, and we shall have no name amongst the iksas of this great nation. Oh! When will this long journey come to an end?"

There were plenty of pine and cypress trees and palmetto; and in a short time the people had constructed sufficient tents to shelter themselves from the rain. Their hunters with but little labor supplied the camps with plenty of bear meat; and the women and children collected quantities of acorns and oksak kapko, and kapun. (large hickory nuts, and scaly barks.) It was an extremely plentiful land, and the whole people were rejoicing at the prospects for a pleasant and bountiful winter. Their camps being completed, the chief gave instructions, to have sufficient ground prepared to plant what seed corn might be found in the camps. Search was made by Isi maleli (running deer) for the corn. He found a few ears only; they had been preserved by the very old people, who had no teeth. The corn they found was two years old, and they were very much afraid that it was dead. The minko, suggested to Isi maleli, that as the tool carriers had iron implements with which to break the ground, it would be best to detail a sufficient number of them, to prepare ground to grow it. So the minko called out twenty of the tool carriers for the purpose, and appointed the wise Isi maleli, to direct them, and to select the soil for growing the corn properly, and to preserve it when it matured.

One end or side of the encampment, lay along the elevated ground—bordering the low lands on the west side of the middle creek. Just above the uppermost camps, and overhanging the creek, was a steep little hill with a hole in one side. As it leaned towards the creek, the people called it the leaning hill (nunih waya). From this little hill the encampment took its name, "Nuni Waya," by which name it is known to this day.

The whole people were healthy at Nunih Waya. Full of life and cheerfulness, they danced and played a great deal. Their scouts had made wide excursions around the encampment, and finding no signs of the enemy in any direction, they consoled themselves with the idea, that they had traveled beyond his reach. The scouts and hunters, on returning into camps, from their exploring expeditions, were often heard to say, "The plentiful, fruitful land of tall trees and running waters, spoken of by our great and wise chiefs, who saw it in a vision of the night, is found. We have found the land of plenty, and our great journey is at an end."

They passed through their first winter at Nunih Waya quite pleasantly. Spring opened finely. Their few ears of corn came up well and grew off wonderfully. The creeks were full of fish, and the mornings rang with the turkeys and singing birds. The woods everywhere were full of buffalo, bear, deer and elks; everything that could be wished for was there, and easily procured. All were filled with gladness.

And when the time for the green corn dance was near, the hunters brought into the camps wonderful quantities of fat meat, and they celebrated this dance five days. They did not eat of their corn, but that it might be properly called the green corn dance, they erected a pine pole in the center of the dance ground, and upon this they suspended a single ear of green corn.

When they had finished this, their forty-third green corn dance in the wilderness, the people began to be concerned as to the probabilities of their having to journey further. Many of them declared that if the sacred pole should indicate a removal, it would be impossible for them to go farther, on acount of the great number of bones that had accumulated on their long journey. They could not carry the bones, neither could they think of leaving them behind.

The chief had for sometime been considering the great inconvenience the marvelous amount of bones had become to the nation. He knew very well, the feelings of the people on the subject, and how difficult it would be to get them to consent to abandon the useless encumbrance. He could see very plainly, that should they have to go further, a portion of the people, under their present impressions in regard to the dry bones, would be most certainly left behind. On hearing the murmuring suggestions of so many of the people, every day, about the bones of their deceased relatives, and

the sacred duty incumbent on the living to preserve and take care
of them, he was convinced that the subject must be approached with
caution. Yet, the oppressive, progress-checking nature of the bur-
dens was such that they must be disposed of in some way.

He called a council of the leaders of the iksas, and in a very prudent and cautious manner, consulted them in behalf of the suffering
people, enquiring of them at the same time, if it was possible to
invent any means that would aid them in the transportation of their
enormous packs of useless dry bones. It was a subject they had not
before thought of, and they required a day or two to make up their
minds.

Time was granted to them, and in the meantime the minko con-
vened with many of the people about it.

The council met again, and there was some discussion, but nothing conclusive. They were loath to speak of the bones of their deceased friends and relatives. They had packed their bones a great
ways, and for years; but there had been no conversation, no consultation, on the subject. There were among the young people, many
who were carrying heavy packs of bones, who had never heard, and
who really did not know whose bones they were carrying. They had
grown up with the bones on their backs, and had packed them faithfully, but never having heard the name of their original owners, they
could tell nothing, nor did they know anything about them. That
the spirits hovered about their bones to see that they were respectfully cared for; and that they would be offended and punished with
bad luck, sickness, or even death for indignities, or neglect of their
bones, every one knew. It was a great indignity to the spirits to repeat
the names they were known by during their mundane existence. The
greater part of the living who were then in the camp, had been born
and reared in the wilderness, and were still packing the bones of
those who had lived long before and of whom they knew nothing.
Yet they worried along with the heavy loads of these dry bones on
their journey, in good faith, and a full belief of its necessity as a
sacred duty. The leaders of the iksas, who were now in council, were
carrying heavy loads of bones themselves which they could not con-

sent to part with; and they esteemed it a subject of too much deli-
cacy to be caviled about in a council. They did not wish to say anything further about it, anyway.

One of the Isht ahullos, who was an old man, and who had long
been a secret teacher, among the women and children, on the nature
and wants of the Spirit world and the causes that made it necessary
to pack the bones of the dead, arose from his seat and said:

> Some people can make very light talk about the bones of our de-
> ceased friends and relatives. Those sacred relics of our loved ones,
> who have passed away from our sight are to be irreverently stigma-
> tized by the name of "oppressive burthen," "useless incumbrance,"
> and the like. Awful! And it was our chief who would dare to apply
> the uncivil epithet to the precious and far-fetched treasures. From
> all these things, I am forced, unwillingly, to infer that the next thing
> the chief has to propose for your consideration will be for you to
> cast away this "oppressive burthen." Shameful! (Hofahya.) This
> thing must not be. This people must not cast away the precious re-
> mains of the fathers and mothers of this nation. They are charged
> by the spirits, who are hovering thick around us now, to take care
> of them; and carry them whithersoever the nation moves. And this
> we must not, we dare not fail to do. Were we to cast away the bones
> of our fathers, mothers, brothers, sister, for the wild dogs to gnaw
> in the wilderness, our hunters could kill no more meat; hunger and
> disease would follow; then confusion and death would come; and
> the wild dogs would become fat on the unscaffolded carcasses of this
> unfeeling nation of forgetful people. The vengeance of the offended
> spirits would be poured out upon this foolish nation.

The council before which the Isht ahullo made this appeal to the
religious sentiment of the tribe was only an assembly of the leaders
of the iksas. The people were not present, and did not hear it. The
chief, however, was fully apprised of the secret action of these bad
men; and to counteract their dark and mischievous influence on the
minds of the people, he dismissed the Isht ahullos, and leaders of
the iksas, with a severe reprimand, telling them plainly that he had
no further business for them to attend to. Then turning to the Isht
ahullo, and at the same time pointing at him with an arrow, said:
"When you again get in council with the lazy, bad hearted men to
which you belong, tell them that the time has come when you must

be cautious how you meddle with the affairs of this nation. Hear my words."

The minko, returning to his tent, sent for Long Arrow, to whom he communicated his designs as to the disposition of the dry bones; after which he directed him to send the tool carriers to the iksas, and instruct them to summon every man, woman and child, except the leaders of the clans and the conjurers of all grades. The minko said: "Tell the people to assemble at the dance ground early in the day, to-morrow. I wish to consult them on important national business. Let the people, except those I have named, all know it before they sleep."

In accordance with the notice sent by the chief, the entire tribe male and female, old and young, except the yushpakammi and the leaders came. These were not found in the great assembly. But the healthy, clean washed, bright, cheerful people were all present, and seated at the time the minko came to his place on the council ground.

The minko looked around on the multitude, and very calmly speaking, addressed them as follows:

It is to you my brothers, my sisters, my countrymen, that I wish to declare my thoughts this day. I look around upon the bright, cheerful countenance of the multitude and I feel assured that you will hear my words; and that you will hearken to my counsels. You are a great people, a wonderful people, a people of strength, of unparalleled courage and untiring, patient industry. Your goodness of heart has caused you to work and hunt, far beyond the needs of your families, to gain a surplus, to feet a lazy, gluttonous set of hangers on, whose aim it is to misdirect you, whose counsels are all false, and whose greatest desire is confusion and discord amongst this peaceful, happy people. I know the meaning of my words. I speak them boldly and intentionally, I do not catch you in a corner, one at a time, and secretly communicate to you messages from the spirit land; packing you with enormous and insupportable burthens, to gratify wicked and discontented spirits, who are, as you are told, hovering about the camps, threatening mischief. But I call you all in general council and standing up in this bright sunlight, with every eye upon me, and declare in language that cannot be mistaken, words of wisdom and truth. I bring no message from the spirit land. I declare to you the needs and interests of the living. I have no visions of the night; no communications from the discontented spirits, who it is said are hovering around our camps, threatening disaster and death to the living, out of spite for having been rejected from the good hunting ground, to tell you of; but openly, in this bright day, I communicate to you, in deepest solicitude, the long cherished thoughts of a live man; which, when fully carried out, cannot fail to establish peace, harmony, concord and much gladness to this great live nation. I speak not to the dead; for they cannot hear my words. I speak not to please or to benefit the dead; there is nought I can do or say, that can by any possibility reach their condition. I speak to the living for the advancement and well being of this great, vigorous, live multitude. Hear my words.

From new motions and indications made by the sacred pole, which I had never witnessed before, I was led to conclude that our forty-three years' journey in an unknown country had come to its termination. And to avoid hindering and annoying the whole people with what I had on my mind to be considered, I called, yesterday (pilashash) a council of the leaders of the iksas, and all the conjurers, for the purpose of examining and deciding on the most prudent course to pursue, in case it should be finally ascertained, that the leader's pole had settled permanently.

They all came, and after hearing my propositions, they put on wise faces, talked a great deal of the unhappy spirits of our dead friends, of their wants and desires, and of the great dangers that would befall the people, if they failed to obey the unreasonable demands made by the spirits, through the lazy Isht ahullos, conjurers and dreamers, who, according to their own words, are the only men through which the spirits can make manifest to the nation their burthensome and hurtful desires. Finding that they had nothing to say, nor did they even surmise anything on the subject of the affairs and interests of the living, I dismissed them as ignorant of, and enemies to the rights of the people, and, therefore, improper agents for the transaction of their business. They were dismissed on account of their secret, malicious designs on the people, and their inefficiency in the councils of the nation. I immediately sent out runners to convene the people in general council to-day. You are all here, except the secret mongers, and the leaders of the clans, whose mouths and tongues have been tied up by the Isht ahullo and yushpakammi. The nation is present to hear my words; in them there is no secret or hidden meaning. You will all hear them, and let everyone, who is a man, open his mouth this clear day, and openly and fearlessly pour out his full and undisguised feelings on the topics which will be presented.

From signs which I have just named, I conclude, and I find it the prevailing impression of this multitude of self-sustaining people, that our long journey of privations and dangers in the pathless wilderness has ended. We are now in the land of tall trees and running waters, of fruit, game of many kinds and fish and fowl, which was spoken of by our good chief, who is missing, in the far off country towards the setting sun. His words have come to pass. Our journey is at an end, and we shall grow to be a nation of happy people in this fruitful land.

Let us now, like a sensible people, put the nation in a suitable condition for the free enjoyment of the inexhaustible bounties that have been so lavishly spread in this vast country for the use and benefit of this multitude. Let us lay aside all useless encumbrance, that we may freely circulate, with our families in this widely extended land, with no burthen to pack, but such as are necessary to sustain life and comfort to our wives and little ones. Let us call this place; this, Nunih Waya encampment, our home; and it shall be so, that when a man at his hunting camp, in the distant forests, shall be asked for his home place, his answer will be, "Nunih Waya." And to establish Nunih Waya more especially as our permanent home, the place to which when we are far away, our thoughts may return with feelings of delight and respectful pleasure, I propose that we shall by general consent and mutual good feelings select an eligible location within the limits of the encampment and there, in the most respectful manner, bring together and pile up in beautiful and tasteful style the vast amount of bones we have packed so far and with which many of the people have been so grievously oppressed. Let each set of bones remain in its sack, and after the sacks are closely and neatly piled up, let them be thickly covered over with cypress bark. After this, to appease and satisfy the spirits of our deceased relatives, our blood kin, let all persons, old and young, great and small, manifest their respect for the dead, by their energy and industry in carrying dirt to cover them up, and let the work of carrying and piling earth upon them be continued until every heart is satisfied. These bones, as we all know, are of the same iska, the same kindred. They were all the same flesh and blood; and for us to pile their bones all in the same heap and securely cover them up will be more pleasing to the spirits, than it will be to let them remain amongst the people, to be scattered over the plains, when the sacks wear out in the hands of another generation who will know but little and care less about them.

You have heard my talk. I have delivered to you the true sentiments of my heart. When it comes to my time to depart for the spirit land, I shall be proud to know that my bones had been respectfully deposited in the great mound with those of my kindred. What says the nation?

Some little time elapsed; and there was no move among them. The multitude seemed to reflect. At length, a good looking man of about sixty winter, arose in a dignified manner, from his seat, and gravely said:

It was in my boyhood, and on the little river where we had the great fish feast, that my much respected father died. His family remained and mourned a whole moon, and when the cry-poles were pulled down, and the feast and dance had ended, my mother having a young child to carry, it fell to my lot, being the next largest member of the family, to pack on the long journey, the bones of my father. I have carefully carried them over hardships and difficulties, from that little rocky river to the present encampment. Such has been my love and respect for these sacred relics, that I was ready at any time to have sacrificed my life sooner than I would have left them, or given them up to another. I am now growing old; and with my declining years come new thoughts. Not long hence, I too must die. I ask myself, who in the coming generations will remember and respect the bones of my father? Will they not be forgotten and scattered to bleach and moulder on the carelessly trodden plain? I have sought with a heart full of anxious sorrow, for a decent and satisfactory resting place, in which to deposit the bones of my long lost father. I could think of none. And I dare assert, that there are thousands in hearing of my voice, at this very moment, whose faithful hearts have asked the same embarrassing questions. I am happy in the acknowledgment, and I trust with much confidence, that the whole people will view this important matter in the same satisfactory light. The wise propositions of our worthy chief have answered perplexing questions and have fuly relieved the unsettled workings of many anxious hearts.

It is true, as our wise chief has already suggested, that we can now witness the wonderful and never before heard of sight of a live nation packing on their backs an entire dead nation, our dead outnumbering the living. It is a pleasure to me, now that my eyes have been opened by the chief's proposition to the propriety of placing these relics of the dead nation to themselves, that we have power and time to do as he suggests, and most reverently to secure them from being tumbled among our greasy packs, and from the occasional dropping of the precious bones, through the holes in the worn-out sacks to be lost forever. Let us, in accordance with the wise and reasonable proposition of our minko, fetch all the sacred relics to one place; pile them up in a comely heap; and construct a mound of earth upon them, that shall protect them from all harm forever.

And the people rose up and with one voice said, "It is well; we are content."

The minko stood up again and said that in that great multitude there might be some whose feelings in regard to the disposition of the bones of their dead friends would not permit them to pile them with the dead nation. Then they all shouted aloud, "It is good, it is satisfactory."

Men were then appointed to select an appropriate place for the mound to be erected on, and to direct the work while in progress. They selected a level piece of sandy land, not far from the middle creek; laid it off in an oblong square and raised the foundation, by piling up earth which they dug up some distance to the north of the foundation. It was raised and made level as high as a man's head and beat down very hard. It was then floored with cypress bark before the work of placing the sacks of bones commenced. The people gladly brought forward and deposited their bones until there were none left. The bones, of themselves, had built up an immense mound. They brought the cypress bark, which was neatly placed on, till the bone sacks were all closely covered in, as dry as a tent. While the tool carriers were working with the bark, women and children and all the men, except the hunters, carried earth continually, until the bark was all covered from sight constituting a mound half as high as the tallest forest tree.

The minko kindled the council fire, and, calling an assembly of the people, told them that the work on the great monumental grave had been prosecuted with skill and wonderful industry. He said that the respect which they had already manifested for the deceased relatives was very great; that notwithstanding the bones were already deeply and securely covered up, the work was not yet completed. Yet it was sufficiently so to allow them to suspend operations for a season. Winter was drawing near; the acorns and nuts were beginning to fall and were wasting. The people must now scatter into the forests and collect the rich autumnal fruits which are showering down from every tree. That done, the people must return to the encampment; and as the tool carriers have produced seed corn enough for all to have a little field, each family must prepare ground for that purpose. Then, after the corn is grown and the new corn feast and dance is celebrated and over, the nation can again prosecute the work on the mound, and so on, from year to year, until the top of the great grave of the dead nation shall be as high as the tallest forest tree. And it shall be made level on the top as much as sixty steps (habli) in length and thirty steps in width,[1] all beat down hard, and planted thick with acorns, nuts and pine seeds. "Remember my words," said the chief, "and finish the work accordingly. Now go and prepare for winter."

And the people gladly dispersed into the distant forests. Fruit was found in great quantities and was collected and brought into camp in very large amounts,—acorns, hickory nuts, and most and best of all, the otupi (chestnuts), all of which was secured from the worms by the process of drying them by smoke and incasing them in small quantities in airtight mud cells in the same manner, that the mud daubers (lukchuk chanuskik) preserve their spiders. Their hunters were very successful; and at midwinter, when all the clans had returned to their camps, they found themselves rich in their supplies of so many things that were good for food, they concluded that as the best way of expressing their unfeigned gratitude (yokoke ahni) to the great sun they would celebrate a grand, glad feast, and joyous dance, before they commenced the work of clearing and breaking ground for their cornfields. So they cleaned out the dance ground, and planted the pole with the golden sun in the center of it. The people collected and, with much joy and gladness of heart, feasted and danced five days.

The amount of ground necessary to plant what corn they had was small, and was soon planted. Then having nothing else to be working at, a thoughtful old man, pointing to the great unfinished mound (yokni chishinto) said, "the weather is cool and pleasant, and the grave of your dead kindred is only half as high as a tall tree." Taking the timely suggestion of the man, thousands went to work, carrying dirt to the great mound. Afterwards, it became an honorable thing to carry and deposit earth on the mound at any time they were not engaged at work in their domestic vocations.

The winter over, spring with its green foliage and singing birds and its grand flourish of gobbling turkeys came slowly on. Corn was planted and the companies of hunters went forth. The camps were healthy. Those who were planting soon finished it, and engaged actively forthwith in throwing earth upon the already huge mound. Their corn flourished well, producing enough, after preserving a portion of their fields for seed, to supply a full feast for the green corn dance.

At the Nunih Waya encampment, everything went well and there were no complaints. Their hunters made wide excursions, acquainted themselves with the geography of the country to the extent of many days' journey around. But, as yet, they had discovered no signs of the enemy, or of any other people. In this happy condition of health and plenty—for they had enlarged their fields and were harvesting abundant crops of corn—years rolled round; the work on the mound was regularly prosecuted; and at the eighth green corn dance celebrated at Nunih Waya, the committee who had been appointed at the commencement, reported to the assembled multitude that the work was completed and the mound planted with the seeds of the forest trees, in accordance with the plan and direction of the minko, at the beginning of the work.

The minko then instructed the good old Lopina, who had carried it so many years, to take the golden sun to the top of the great mound and plant it in the center of the level top.

When the people beheld the golden emblem of the sun glittering on the top of the great work which, by the united labor of their own hands, had just been accomplished, they were filled with joy and much gladness. And in their songs at the feast, which was then going on, they would sing: "Beyond the wonderful work of our hands; and let us be glad. Look upon the great mound; its top is above the trees, and its black shadow lies on the ground, a bow-shot. It is surmounted by the golden emblem of the sun; its glitter (tohpakali) dazzles the eyes of the multitude. It inhumes the bones of fathers and relatives; they died on our sojourn in the wilderness. They died in a far off wild country; they rest at Nunih Waya. Our journey lasted many winters; it ends at Nunih Waya."

The feast and the dance, as was the custom, continued five days. After this, in place of the long feast, the minko directed that, as a mark of respect due to the fathers and mothers and brothers and sisters, for whom they had with so much labor prepared such a beautiful and wonderfully high monumental grave, each iksa should come to the mound and, setting up an ornamental pole for each clan, hold a solemn cry a whole moon. Then, to appease the restless spirits of the deceased nation and satisfy all the men and women with what they had done with the sacred relics of their dead, the Choctaws held a grand and joyous national dance and feast for two days. And returning to their tents, they remembered their grief no more.

All the people said that their great chief was full of wisdom; that his heart was with the people; and that his counsels had led them in the clean and white paths of safety and peace. Each of the iksas selected very tall pine poles, which they peeled and made white and ornamented with festoons of evergreens and flowers. Then in most solemn form, they performed the cry three times every day, during one whole moon. Then at the great national pole pulling, they celebrated a grand feast and dance of two days. The rejoicing of the nation was very great, and they returned to their camps with glad hearts, remembering their sorrows no more.

Afterward, when a death occurred, and the bones had been properly cleansed, they were deposited in a great cavity which had been constructed for that purpose, as the work of the mound was progressing. It was the national sepulchral vault; and thither the bones of all the people that died at Nunih Waya were carried and neatly-stored away in dressed leather sacks. Thus arose the custom of burying the dead in the great monumental sepulchre. And when a member of a hunting party of more than two men or a family died, too far out in the forest to pack home the bones, which could not be cleaned in the woods,—for the bone pickers never went hunting—it was deemed sufficient to appease the wandering spirit to place all his hunting implements close to the dead body, just as death had left it. In such cases it was not lawful to touch the dead, and they were covered with a mound of earth thirty steps in circumference and as high as a man's head. If death occurred at the camp of an individual family in the far off hunt, the survivors would, during the cry moon, carry, in cane baskets and the blade bones of the buffalo, a sufficient amount of earth to construct a mound of the above dimensions. If there should be but two men at a camp, or a lone man and his wife, and one should die, the survivor had to carry the dead body home. Life for life, was the law; and every life had to be accounted for in a satisfactory manner. It would not answer for a man to return home and report that his hunting companion or his wife had been lost or drowned, devoured by wild beasts or died a natural death. He must show the body. There are occasionally found among the great number of tumuli scattered over the land, mounds of larger dimensions than ordinary ones. These mounds were constructed by females. Upon the death in camp of a man who had an affectionate wife, his mourning tekchi (wife), regardless of the customary time to cry, would throw down her hair and with all her strength and that of her children would carry earth, and build upon the mound as long as they could find food of any kind that would sustain life. They would then return to camp, worn out skeletons.

Now, my white friend, I have explained to you the origin, and who it was that built the great number of mounds that are found scattered over this wide land. The circular, conic mounds are all graves, and mark the spot where the persons, for whom they were built, breathed their last breath. There being no bone pickers at the hunting camps to handle the dead, the body was never touched, or moved from the death posture. Just as it lay, or sat, as the case might be, it was covered up, first with either stones, pebbles, or sand, and finished off with earth. In this way the custom of mound graves originated from the great mound graves, Nunih Waya, and it prevailed with the Choctaw people until the white man came with his destructive, sense-killing "fire water," and made the people all drunk.

After getting in possession of this information, in regard to the origin and make of the mounds, I took pains to excavate quite a number of them, which were found on the "second flat" along the Tombecbee river. They contained invariably a single human skeleton. The bones generally, except the skull, were decomposed. The crania of most of them would bear handling, when first taken out, but when exposed to the air they too soon fell to ashes. Along with the ashes of the bones, in most cases, would be found five or six arrow points, a stone ax, and not infrequently a stone skin-dresser. In all cases, the bones would be found enveloped, sometimes lying on the side, feet drawn up; at other times in a sitting posture, either in sand, pebbles, or small stones. In one or two cases, the coals and the charred ends of the pine knots that lighted up the last sad night of the deceased, lay in front and near the bones, under the sand.

As soon as the national cry was over, the poles pulled down, and the great dance celebrated, the families dispersed into the far off hunting grounds where they enjoyed the game and fruits, until midwinter; when they returned to their homes to prepare and put their fields in order for the coming planting time. The seasons at Nunih Waya were good every year; and they had on hand corn in abundance. Their mode of putting it away, in small lots, in air tight earthen cells, preserved it, from year to year, for an indefinite period, as sound and as fresh as new corn. To keep it dry and entirely excluded from the air, was all that was necessary, to preserve it for any length of time, in the same condition in which it was when put up.

Feeling themselves permanently settled after the mound was completed, they planted larger crops and were beginning to construct good, dry houses in which to dwell. The next year after the mound was finished, having a very large crop of corn, they celebrated the green corn dance, eating nothing besides the corn. On the first day of the feast, and at the time the people had assembled to receive instructions in regard to the manner of conducting the ceremonies, the minko came upon the dance ground, and calling the attention of the multitude said:

We are a brave and exceedingly prosperous people. We are an industrious people. We till the ground in large fields, thereby producing sustenance for this great nation. We are a faithful and dutiful people. We packed the bones of our ancestors on our backs, in the wilderness, forty-three winters, and at the end of our long journey piled up to their memory a monument that overshadows the land like a great mountain. We are a strong, hardy, and very shifty people. When we set out from the land of our fathers, the Chata tribe numbered a little less than nineteen thousand. We have traveled over a pathless wilderness, beset with rocks, high mountains, sun-scorched plains, with dried up rivers of bitter waters; timbered lands and mighty streams of swift waters; dark shadowy low-lands, full of lakes and ferocious wild beasts. Bravely we have battled and triumphed over all. We have not failed, but are safely located in the rich and fruitful land of tall trees and running brooks seen in a vision of the night, and described by our good chief who is missing. And we number now a little more than twenty-one thousand. Assuredly we are a wonderful people. A people of great power. A united, friendly people irresistibly strong (hlampko).

Then turning and pointing with his hand, he said:

Behold the sacred pole, the gift of the Great Spirit. To it we are to attribute all our success. When the enemy pursued on our track, its truthful indications gave us timely notice to escape from danger. When we wavered in the trackless desert it leaned and led us onward in the paths of safety. When we reached the swift, wide river, it bowed its ominous head; we crossed to Nunih Waya. Here it danced and made many motions, but did not indicate for us to go further. As a leading light to our feet and as a great power, it has conducted us from the far distant West (hush ai akatula) to the rising sun; to the land of safety and plenty. It is a sacred relic of our pilgrimage in the unknown regions. As such we must preserve it for the coming generations to see and remember the potent leader of their fathers in the wilderness. It is proposed by the wise Isht ahullo, who has faithfully carried the sacred pole ever since the virtuous and ingenious Peni ikbi died, that a circular mound, forty steps in circumference at the base, as high as once and a half the length of the sacred pole, be erected eastward from the great monument, on the high ground towards the middle creek; and that inasmuch as your good, lazy Isht ahullos, yushpakammi, dreamers, spirit talkers and medicine men, did not find it convenient to assist you in the construction of the great monument for the dead nation, let them be required to construct with their own hands, this mound for the leader's pole to rest on. They pretend to be always dealing with spirits and sacred things, and no other men should be allowed to work on the mound, that is to constitute a resting place for the sacred pole. The work must be performed and finished by the sacred conjurers, in accordance with the plan and directions of the wise Isht ahullo, who carries the leader's pole, and who is this day appointed to superintend the work.

The pole-bearing Isht ahullo, marked off the ground, and placing the sacred pole in the center of it, summoned the whole of the conjurers and sorcerers to commence the work. They came, but they were so extremely awkward and lazy that the work progressed quite slowly. The Isht ahullo, who was superintendent of the work, exerted his whole power to encourage them to facilitate the building of the mound. It was all to no effect. They grumbled from morning till night and moved so slowly at their work, that a child could have done as much work as they accomplished in a day. The superintendent shortened their daily supply of food. They did less work and grumbled more. He made their daily food still less. They, with but few exceptions, ran off into the woods, and scattering themselves among the camps of the hunters, sponged upon them until the hunters, becoming tired of them, drove them from their camps like dogs. They returned to Nunih Waya, but did not resume their work. The superintendent of the work complained to the chief. The chief called the tool carriers and instructed them to go out and select a piece of land, that would not interfere with the claims of the iksas; lay out a plot of land, twenty steps square for each one of the yushpakammi, who is not found engaged at work on the mound; and set the idle conjurers to work on it, preparing the ground to plant corn. We are settled permanently now, and every member of the nation, who is healthy, must perform sufficient labor to produce, at least, as much food and raiment as he consumes. This people shall not labor and sweat to support a lazy, heartless set of men, whose only duty is falsehood, and whose influence disturbs the quiet of the nation. The tool carriers laid off the little plats of land, but the conjurers paid no attention to the order for them to work it. The chief then appointed a day for the people to meet in council for the purpose of taking into consideration the bad character of these lazy men and the demoralizing influence they exerted in the nation. The whole number of the conjurers were also summoned to attend the council and defend their rights to enjoy all the privilege of the camps, with entire exemption from labor or any visible calling.

On the day appointed for the council, all the people who were out hunting came. But of the spirit talkers and conjurers, there were not exceeding thirty in the assembly, and they were all known to be industrious men. Messengers were sent to warn them to the council. They were not to be found in the camps; and it was discovered that a great number of women were missing. The assembly immediately broke up and parties were sent out to capture and bring home the women at least.

After several days diligent search, the parties all returned and reported that the conjurers must have gone off on the wind; for they could discover no trace nor sign of them in any direction. Nor did they ever know certainly what went with them.

At the time this thing occurred there were so many people absent from the encampment that they were unable to make an estimate of the number that were missing but from the number of children, left without mothers in the camp, it was known to be very considerable. As far as could be ascertained, they were the wives of men, without exception, who were out hunting. It was distressing to see the great number of small children who were running to and fro in the camps, and to hear their incessant lament. "Sa ishka muto" (Where is my mother) was heard in all directions. They were mostly small children, and generally of young mothers who had abandoned both them and their absent husbands and run off with the lazy conjuring priests and medicine men.

At midwinter, when the hunting parties had all returned, an effort was made to ascertain the number of women who had left their families to follow the conjurers and priests. From the best computation they could make, the number was nearly two hundred, and it so much excited the bereaved husbands and the people generally, against the Isht ahullo and conjurers of every grade, that it was with much difficulty the minko found himself able to dissuade them from falling upon the few that were left, and who were faithfully at work on the mound. In their rage, they protested that the whole mass of lazy Isht ahullo, conjurers, spirit talkers, and medicine men were all alike, enemies to the men that fed them and seducers and prostitutors of the women who clothed them. They declared that there was no good in them, and that they ought not to live. This manifestation of the low, gross nature of the priests and conjurers, depreciated their standing with the whole people. It sank them to a degree of infamy and suspicion from which they have never recovered. To this day they are pushed aside in decent company, and looked upon with scorn and contempt.

The Isht Ahullo, who was so long the bearer of the sacred pole, had always deported himself as a good, industrious man; and it was from his management that the investigation of their conduct, and the flights of the conjuring priests had been brought about. After a time with the small band of Isht ahullos that had been left, he completed the mound in good style, and planting the sacred pole permanently on its top, he desired the chief to call the nation to its examination, and if the work met with the approbation of the people, he wish them to receive it, and discharged him and his workmen from further duties in regard to the sacred pole.

When the people came, they gave their approbation of the comely proportions of the mound by a long continued shout. And by another uproarous shout congratulated themselves on the certainty that their long journey in the wilderness had most assuredly ended. At this, the sacred pole began jumping up and punching itself deeper and deeper into the ground, until it went down slowly out of sight into the mound. At witnessing the wonderful manifestation of the settling pole, there were no bounds to their rejoicings, and they danced and brought provisions, making a glad celebration that continued three days and nights on the occasion of the departing sacred pole.

Having sufficient ground cleared to produce as much bread as they needed, and a large surplus, the people had time to construct houses to dwell in and to keep their surplus provisions dry and safe. They constructed their houses of earth at Nunih Waya, and that fashion prevailed until the white people came to live in the nation with them.

The larger game was becoming scarcer and the hunters were extending their excursions wider. The people, however, were producing such abundant supplies of corn that they did not require a very great amount of meat and the hunters were extending their explorations more for the purpose of becoming acquainted with a wide range of country and for their own satisfaction than from necessity. Time rolled on, the people were healthy, and had increased at a very great ratio. They had extended their settlements up the Nunih Waya creek, and out in the country between Nunih Waya and Tuli Hikia creeks, to half a day's journey; and they were growing corn over the entire district.

About thirty winters after they had stopped at Nunih Waya, a party of hunters who had progressed a little further north than usual, fell in with a camp of hunters belonging to the Chickasha tribe. After finding that they spoke the same language with themselves, the Chahtas approached their camp in a friendly manner, and remained several days. The older men amongst them being familiar with the traditional history of the journeyings of their respective tribes, took much pleasure in communicating to each other an account of their travels. From the point where the two tribes separated, the Chickashas diverged widely to the left, found an extremely rough and scarce country for some time, but at length emerging from the mountains on to the wide spread plains, they found the buffalo and other game plentiful. They continued to travel, with only an occasional halt, to rest the women and feeble ones, until they came to the great river, at the place called by them, sakti ahlopulli (bluff crossing)—white people call is now Chickasaw Bluffs, said the old man. They made shift to cross the great river, and traveling onward, the leader's pole came to a stand at a place now called Chickasha Old Town in a high and beautiful country. The leader's pole stood at this place three winters, at the end of which time the pole was found leaning to the northeast. They set out again, and crossed another big river (little prairie, near Huntsville, Alabama). The pole remained there erect only one winter. At mulberry time the ensuing summer the pole was found leaning almost directly to the south. They packed up, and crossing many bold running rivers, the pole still leading onward, until they came to a large river, near where it emptied into the great okhuta (ocean). At this beautiful country (below where Savannah, Georgia, now stands) the pole stood erect many winters. The fish, opa haksum, oka folush (oysters, clams) and all manner of shell fish and fowl, and small game were plentiful. The people obtained full supplies of provisions with but little labor. In the process of time, however, the people became sickly, and they were visited with a very great plague. They called the plague hoita lusa (black vomit) because the people died, vomiting black matter, resembling powdered fire coals and fish slime. All that took it were sick but a day or two and died so fast that the people became frightened and ran off, leaving great numbers of the dead unburied. They followed the leader's pole back nearly over the same route they went, until finally they returned to the place where the pole made its first stand (Chickasha Old Towns). Here it stood again, and remained erect until it rotted.

After the Chahtas had found where their brother Chickashas had located, they paid occasional visits to their country. But the Chickashas becoming suspicious that the Chahtas were seeking some advantage, gave them orders not to extend their hunts north of a certain little river. The Chahtas paid no attention to the proclamation sent by the Chickashas, and it turned out that the Chickashas attacked and killed three or four of their hunters who had camped north of the interdicted river.

When the news reached Nunih Waya, the people were grieved; for they had felt proud of finding their Chickasha brethren and were preparing to cultivate their friendship. The minko, thinking it possible that there might be some mistake in the matter, sent an embassy to the chief of the Chickasha nation, to ascertain the cause of the murderous conduct of his hunters. The Chickasha chief ordered the Chahta embassy to be scourged and sent back with no other answer. The Chahtas were very much enraged. They had received an indignity that they could not account for; and they felt mortified in the extreme. The Chahta chief did not feel willing to go to war with them, and made up his mind to give orders to his hunters to abstain from hunting beyond the river named by the Chickashas. But before he had time to carry his peace plans into action, all the hunters north of Nunih Waya had been attacked at their camps on the hunting grounds. Great numbers of the men had been killed, and their women carried off captive. Those hunters who had escaped from the attacked camps reported that the Chickashas were very numerous, and that their warriors were very large and overpowering in battle. The present generation of the Chahta people had never seen any people but their own tribe; and the news of the captured women, murdered hunters and the vast hordes of rushing irresistible warriors that were pouring down into their hunting grounds from the Chickasha country, had frightened the Chahta people into a fearful panic. Some of them had already proposed to evacuate their comfortable homes at Nunih Waya and seek some safer country for their wives and little ones to dwell in. But they did not ponder the matter long. The spies coming in, reported that great numbers of the Chickashas had their camps, and were killing up the game in two days' travel of Nunih Waya.

The Chahta minko kindled the council fire; and calling a national council, submitted for their consideration the whole matter of the Chikasha depredations; and called upon them to investigate the subject and decide on the proper course to pursue in the case. The people promptly assembled and were confessedly very much alarmed. Some of the young warriors moved that the Chahta people should rise at once and kill every Chickasha they could find within the limits of their hunting grounds. Others who were not quite so fiery thought that a precipitate move on the part of the Chahtas would only bring disaster, while there were others who advocated immediate flight as the only chance for safety.

At length, old Long Arrow, who had always been leader of the tool carriers, arose and said:

I am old now, and cannot, if I desired, make much of a flight. I shall remain at Nunih Waya. My bones shall sleep in the great mound. I am also opposed to precipitate movements. Let us prepare plenty of arms and make systematic movements. Let us organize one hundred companies, with ten active men in each, and a prudent, brave warrior to lead each company. Let these hundred companies be sent forward immediately, with instructions to examine and ascertain the force and position of the enemy; but not to make battle, except when they are attacked. Let them stay a long time, and be seen in many places, as by accident, in the day time; but at night, let them scatter and sleep without fire in dark places. In the meantime, let all those who remain in the encampment go to work and throw up a high circular earth wall that shall include the two mounds and space enough to contain all the women and children, as well as the aged and infirm, in case of a siege. All this completed and all the corn and other provisions that can be had stored away inside of the great wall, we shall be ready to increase our forces; hunt down the enemy and scalp them wherever they may be found.

The multitude breathed easier and looked brighter. The minko then spoke to the people, giving them great encouragement. He said:

The great war talk of the long tried friend of the people, Long Arrow, is full of wisdom, and his words brace the flagging spirits of the nation. His counsels lead to safety, and his instructions and plans to victory. Let the people not hesitate. Turn out your hundred companies of warriors. Send them out immediately. Appoint wise men to lay off and direct the work on the earth wall and let all that can carry a load of dirt as large as his head be found busily engaged from day to day, until the wall is completed. Be industrious. Let every one do his duty in this great work. Let all the people be brave and faithful and danger cannot approach you.

And the people answered and said: "It is a good talk. Lay off the ground; we are ready for the work; it shall rise up as a cloud in a summer's day."

The companies were organized the same day and took their departure the next day. Men were appointed to lay off and superintend the work on the earthen wall. The people, old and young, stringing themselves around the entire circle, threw up the earth from the outside of the wall to the height of two men, in eight days. And they left two gaps in the wall, of five steps each. One at the east and the other at the west, for the ingress and egress of the people[2] which they did not intend to close until Nunih Waya should be actually invaded by the enemy.

The minko then organized his whole effective force and ordered them to make arrows and war clubs as fast as possible and bring them into the mound of the sacred pole, where he had a house erected, in which to deposit them.

Notes

1. I visited this celebrated mound in 1843. I found it rounded off, oblong square, 200 yards in circumference at its base; 80 feet in height, with a flat space on the top 52 yards in length by 25 yards in width, the whole mound was thickly set with large forest trees. 200 yards to the north of it is a lake, which I supposed to be the place whence they carried the earth to construct the mound.

2. I went all round this earth wall in 1843. It seemed to be a complete circle, and from one and a half to two miles in circumference, the southeastern portion cutting the bluff of Nunih Waya creek. Many places in the wall were still eight feet in height. The two gaps in the wall had never been filled up.

LIFE OF APUSHIMATAHA

Gideon Lincecum

DURING THE FOUR YEARS, 1822, 23, 24 and 25, I resided in the Chahta country; I became acquainted with the chiefs of the three districts, into which the nation was divided, and quite a number of their leaders, headmen and warriors.[1]

At that time Mushulatubi, Apushimataha and Apukshinubi, were the chiefs of the three districts which had been established long before my acquaintance with that noble people commenced. Each district was subdivided, with but little system, into Iksas, or kindred clans, and each of these Iksas had its leader. All the men seemed to be warriors, and they had their captains and generals, which titles they had learned from the white people, for whom they always professed, and indeed manifested, the greatest friendship. I remember now, though the time has long past, with feelings of unfeigned gratitude the many kindnesses bestowed on me and my little family in 1818 and 1819, while we were in their neighborhood, before the country began to fill up with other white people. Some of them would visit us almost every day and seemed quite proud that the white people were about to become their neighbors. Until I had raised a crop of corn we procured all our provisions from our Chahta neighbors, on very good terms. I did not then understand their language, but their negroes whom they had purchased from the white people did, and we used them for interpreters in our business transactions. It affords me pleasure now, after the lapse of near half a century, to recall in memory the many happy days and hours I spent in the days of my young manhood in friendly intercourse with that innocent and unsophisticated people. We met often, hunted together, fished together, swam together, and they were positively, and I have no hesitation in declaring it here, the most truthful, most reliable and best people I have ever dwelt with.

While we resided in their country my wife had a very severe spell of fever, that confined her to her bed for several weeks. During her sickness the good, kind-hearted Chahta women would come often, bringing with them their nicely prepared tampulo water for her to drink, and remaining by the sick bed for hours at a time, would manifest the deep sympathy they felt, by groaning for the afflicted one, all the time of their protracted visit.

The time is long gone, and I may never have the pleasure of meeting with any of that most excellent race of people again. But so long as the life pendulum swings in this old time shattered bosom I shall remember their many kindnesses to me and mine, with sentiments of kindest affection and deepest gratitude, and my prayers for their elevation and progress as a people among the enlightened nations of the earth shall not cease.

I might here record many incidents of thrilling interest that occurred during the time of my familiarity with this noble tribe of aboriginal Americans, but as I set out in this little appendix to note a few facts that came under my observation in regard to the history of their war chiefs and a few of their conspicuous headmen, I must forbear saying more on the minor subjects.

The chiefs of the three districts were elected every four years. All the time I was acquainted with the political action of the nation by re-election the same man held the office of chief. Their elections were conducted *viva voce*, or rather by acclamation, and managed by the people, the candidates having no hand in it, or any knowledge of who the candidates were, until the name of the chief elect was proclaimed by runners among the Iksas.

Mushulatubi was the principal chief, and he held that title many years, until the Chahtas were removed west of the Mississippi; where he died. He was a handsome man, about six feet in height and quite corpulent. He possessed a lively, cheerful disposition, and as all fat men, was good-natured and would get drunk. He was not much of an orator, and to remedy that deficiency he had selected an orator to speak for him. His name was Aiahokatubi, and, except Apushimataha, he could deliver himself more gracefully and with more ease than any man I ever heard address an audience.

Mushuslatubi was a frequent visitor at my house, while I resided in the nation, for it was in his district I had my house, and but eighteen miles from his residence. He was good company, full of agreeable anecdote and witty, inoffensive repartee, until he became too much intoxicated. Then he was nothing but a drunken Indian.

Mushulatubi was not very wealthy. Having but a moderate stock of cows and horses and five or six negroes. He was, however, certainly rich in his family relations. He had a house full of chil-dren and two handsome wives, who, like himself, were healthy and somewhat corpulent. They all dwelt together in the same house, and seemed to be very happy. One of his wives was a quarter white blood and had been, in her young days, quite pretty. He was in the habit, when visited by white people, of pointing out his pretty, fair-skinned wife, and bragging a little. But to an accurate observer it was easily seen that his confidence and his affections rested with the full blooded Chahta wife. She, however, possessed the strongest and best intellect, and to her management of the household affairs the fair-skinned beauty seemed to yield without hesitation.

Mushulatubi resided on the military road, which, previous to the advent of steamboats on the Mississippi River, was the great thoroughfare upon which returned the hosts of flatboat men from Ohio, Kentucky, Tennessee, and Indiana. They were mostly foot-men, who, after disposing of their cargo of produce at New Orleans, came up through the Chahta country on their way to their respec-tive States. I have often heard those weary footmen while passing my house—I also resided on the military road—speaking of the friendly demeanor and the kind hospitality they had received at the house of Mushulatubi.

It sometimes happened that the Ohio traveler would waylay and rob the Kentuckians and Tennesseans within the limits of Mushulatubi's district. On hearing of the robbery he would raise his warriors, rush out in pursuit and never fail to arrest and bring the culprit to Columbus.

Apuckshinubi, who was chief of the district westerly from Mushulatubi's district, was a very different man. He was a large man, tall and bony, had a down look and was of the religious or superstitious cast of mind. He was, by the people of his district, called a good man, and it was said that he was a man of deep thought and that he was quite intellectual. His studiously maintained taciturnity however concealed from my observation that portion of his attributes. But I did not see him often, and my opportunities for making observations in detail on the characteristic traits of the big old ugly chief were not sufficient to enable me to speak decidedly as to the truth or falsehood of his reporters. The people of his district kept him long in the office of chief, and notwithstanding his grum looks and taciturn demeanor, I feel willing to leave him where rumor placed him, an intelligent, good man and a brave, daring warrior. I know nothing of his domestic relations and cannot say whether his couch was or not blessed with one, or a plurality of wives.

The great man of the nation and of the age was the far famed Apushimataha. He was about five feet ten inches in height, stood very erect, full chest, square, broad shoulders and fine front and elevated top head. His mouth was very large, lips rather thick, eyes and nose very good, projecting brow, and cheek bones very prominent. He lacked a great deal of being what the world calls handsome. But he had that inexplicable attribute about him which belongs only to the truly great, that which forced the ejaculation, "who is that?" from all observant strangers. He died at Washington City in December, 1824 (I speak from recollection), and at his own special request was buried with the honors of war. It was the express opinion of his friends at home when they heard of the request and distinguished honors manifested by the white people at the funeral of their deceased warrior chief, that his satisfied "shilombish" had passed away to the good hunting ground without looking back.

I passed his house soon after the news of his decease had reached
the nation; great numbers of families had collected there; had set
up and ornamented many poles and were holding a great "cry" for
their much loved chief. Though he had no blood kin that any one
knew of, nearly all the people of his district claimed him as a relative,
consequently there were many poles set up at the "cry" they were
celebrating for him.

Apushimataha was chief of the district lying south of Mushulatubi's, and he had lived a long way from where I resided. I was never
at his place until after his death. But he visited Mushulatubi's district two or three times a year, and while in that region he seldom
failed to pay me a visit, and remained with me sometimes as much
as two or three weeks.

I may not be a proper judge of such matters, but really I always
looked upon him as possessing the strongest and best balanced intellect of any man I had ever heard speak. I think so yet, although
forty years of great men and their written thoughts have passed between that period and the present Sunday night. At their national
councils quite a number of white men would attend, and I have seen
them, when Apushimataha was the speaker, chained to their seats
for hours at a time, although they understood not a word of his
language. Such was the force of his attitude and expressive gesticulation. His figures and elucidations were sublime beyond comparison. I never shall forget the impression that he made and the change
that he produced by one short speech, upon the minds of quite a
crowd of reckless boatsmen and other rowdy associates, at a council
that was held under a grove of shady oaks near where I lived in the
nation.

I had a man by the name of Luther Parker, a yankee, hired, and
not having sufficient confidence in him to permit him to sleep in
the storehouse, I had attached a little room to the outside of it,
where he slept, for the double purpose of guarding the store and
being convenient to the ferry, which he kept for me. I had furnished
him with a large musket pistol, which he kept over the door of his
little bedroom. After he had been there long enough to obtain a
smattering of the Chahta language he got in the habit of sitting up

of nights, with the Indians, who were nearly always camped around my place, for the purpose of drinking with them. One night we heard a loud gun down at the store, and very soon the Indians were observed to be rapidly running off from the place. While they were running along the road and passing the dwelling house, a Chickasa woman, who happened to be there, came to the window and told me that Louie—as the Indians called my ferryman—had got drunk, had been trying to sell a pistol which he said he had in his little house, to Atoba, who was the brother to the chief Mushulatubi. Atoba was also drunk, and said he did not want to buy a pistol, but the drunken Louie would have him to go and look at it, and when they came together, talking about the pistol, Louie went in and presently handed the pistol to Atoba, who was standing in the bright moonshine, outside of the house, and at the instant that Atoba took hold of the handle of the pistol it exploded and instantly killed the white man Louie. On being asked why, if it was an accident, they were all running so, she replied, "Because they are all frightened at the thought of having killed one of your family."

I went immediately down to the store and found the young man lying with his feet at the door and dead, as the Chickasa woman had said. On further examination I discovered that the contents of the pistol had lodged in his neck, which was broken. Having no other white man about me, and the Indians being all gone, I seated myself on a barrel near the door to wait for the morning. About two hours before day two Indian men came to me and wanted some powder and a ball to fit the pistol. They said Atoba had sent them for it, and that he intended to die at 12 o'clock the ensuing day, by the same pistol with which he had in his drunkenness accidentally killed his white friend. If it was really an accident, I inquired, why will he have himself shot? They replied, life for life is the law, and accidents are not provided for. When I asked who is to do the shooting? One of the men promptly replied, "that honor falls to my lot." I did not furnish them with the ammunition and they hastened away, telling me that they knew where they could procure it, that Atoba was a man and a warrior, not afraid to die, and that I should hear that he did die at the time appointed.

Morning came, and seeing some men who had slept on their boats at the river, I called to them; they came, and while we were washing and shrouding the dead man the two Indians came again and informed me that Atoba had succeeded in procuring powder and lead; that they had hammered out a ball to fit the pistol and that Atoba would die at the middle of the day. They desired me to be satisfied, for he would be sure to die at that time, and they galloped immediately away, not giving me time to reply.

When I told the boatmen what the Indians said they seemed to be highly delighted, and they sent one of their number over to the other town to tell the other boatmen and the town people to come over and witness the pleasing affair. By 10 o'clock quite a number of white people had crossed the river and were streaming along the road to the place of the expected execution.

Atoba had his spies out, and when they informed him of the great number of white people that were pressing forward, manifesting so much eagerness to witness his misfortune, he sent a man to tell me that so many of the white people had crossed the river and were hurrying forward to see him die and to laugh at his sorrowful condition, he had concluded to die at another place, and for me not to be uneasy, that he was not trying to evade or escape from justice. He had forfeited his right to live, and that he would be certain to die as soon as he could get far enough from the white people to prevent them from the pleasing gratification they expected to enjoy on seeing it. And so when they came to the place they were greatly mortified to find that Atoba was not there. They returned, cursing and foaming, and swearing that they would kill every Indian in the nation, and they went over to Columbus to arm and prepare themselves for the slaughter.

All this time I was busily engaged with the dead. They had all turned to warriors and had left me to make arrangements for the funeral as best I could alone.

Soon again the boatmen and such loose characters as they could find about the liquor shops returned, all armed and equipped for the Indian campaign. While I was carrying the dead man over the river to the Columbus graveyard, the army, numbering about fifty men, all half drunk, were passing the river the other way, champing and gnashing their teeth for blood. They marched hurriedly onward, uttering the fierce, horrid yelp of the frantic inebriate and continuing their course to the prairie, about three miles off, where a number of women and children were at that time picking strawberries. On hearing the terrible hooting and yelping of the drunken host the women and their little ones took fright and fled to the thick forests. The double sighted, cross-eyed braves of the furious army caught a glimpse as they fled of the multitudinous maneuvering warriors of the Chahta forces, and, firing off a few of their guns, beat a retreat. They returned, flushed with their success, the same evening, and crossing back to town, drank and sang war songs through the night. So ended the only war ever waged by the American people against the Chahtas.

I had sent Atoba word not to die until I could get time to see him. I had, by the time the corpse was ready for the funeral, seen and talked with several of the women who were present when the accident occurred, and finding clearly that there was no intention on the part of Atoba of killing the man, I was desirous of saving the unfortunate Indian if I could. And for that reason I had sent him word to suspend the dying until I could see him. Accordingly on the next morning after the termination of the *war* I received a message, before sunup, instructing me to go down the military road about half a mile, to a large black pine stump and remain there until a signal should be given. I had been at the stump but a short time when the signal for me to turn square off into the thick woods was given. I had not progressed in the tangled thicket exceeding 100 yards until I came in sight of Atoba, who was sitting on a log, in company with six other Indians, all armed with rifles and scalping knives. As soon as the unfortunate Atoba discovered my approach, he rose from his seat on the log and advanced to meet me, holding the pistol in his hand. When he came near he presented the pistol, breach foremost, and said, "This is the little gun, with which, in my drunkenness, I unfortunately destroyed the life of your man Louie. It is right that I should die for him. Life for life is the law. His unhappy *shilombish* will not be satisfied, nor can it pass to the good hunting ground until I atone with my life for destroying his. I am a man and a warrior, and can die without fear. I am not alive now because I am afraid to die, but because, for reasons of your own, you sent word for me not to die until you could see me. I have obeyed your voice, and have remained until now. You have seen me and I am ready to die. It was your man that I have killed. You are now the avenger. For, inasmuch as you prevented me from dying at the time I had myself appointed, and my friend who was to have performed the last and greatest act of kindness for me has gone away, it devolves on you to do the shooting or appoint some other brave man with a strong heart and steady hand to do it for you. Take the pistol, I am now ready."

I received the pistol and told him to give up his notions about the necessity of dying. I further told him that I had seen and conversed with several persons who were present when the man was killed, from whom I had ascertained that the firing of the pistol was purely accidental, and that I knew of a better way to dispose of the case than for me or any one else to shoot him; that we would go to the United States interpreter and make a paper that would be satisfactory to everybody on the subject. He agreed that such a paper might be made, and that it might relieve and satisfy the minds of the living, but he had done nothing to them, and, besides, it was not the living with whom he had to deal. It was to the wandering, unsatisfied *Shilup* of the man that had been killed, that he was to make atonement, and no paper that could be made would answer that purpose. But he would go with me to John Pichlynn's, United States interpreter, for he, having been raised among the Chahtas from his infancy, was familiar with all their laws and customs, the most particular and best of which was "life for life," would soon explain it to me, and show me that there is no chance for an honorable escape from death in a case like his. From where we then were to John Pitchlynn's was eight miles over a rough woodland country, and the weather was quite warm. We had no horses, I, however, did not return home, but set out on foot with them; we found Pitchlynn at home and had quite a council of it. There were three or four steady old Indians at Pitchlynn's when we arrived; who joined the seven I had with me in the argument that ensued against the United States interpreter and myself, and it was not until we had read from the journal of the Mississippi Legislature that Chahtas had been incorporated as citizens of the State, and that if he got any one to shoot him, whether red or white man, it would lay the shooter liable to trial for murder and that he would be hung for it. After much discussion the Chahtas reluctantly gave up the point on condition that the papers should be so worded as to allow Atoba, in case he should be condemned at the trial before a court of white men, the privilege of being shot, in place of being "weighed" like a dog. They called hanging a man "weighing" him.

I drew up an ordinary appearance bond, with a penalty of $6,000, including the condition, that if condemned at trial, that he should not be "weighed." And also, that the court should consist of five justices of the peace and, at his special request, that the decision of the court of five magistrates in his case should be final. He also required, for the purpose of giving him time to pay his debts, and settling up his business, that the trial be put off thirty days; at which time he would be ready to meet the white judges at any place *in* the Chahta country I might see proper to designate. So I finished up the bond, delaying the trial one month; to take place at the before mentioned grove of oaks, two miles from where the accident occurred. Atoba signed it, with John Pitchlynn and several of the Indians who were present for securities.

I had been gone all day; and when I returned at night, I went over to town, and found the whole people laboring under great excitement. There were at that time not exceeding five hundred men in fifty miles around Columbus able to bear arms. Rumor had already in the field an army of a thousand Indians, which was hourly increasing. All could see, now that it was too late, that by permitting the drunken boatmen, and their grogshop associates, to go over the river the day before, had been bad management; that the Indians had been imprudently and unnecessarily insulted; that in the weak and sparsely settled condition of the country, it would be an easy matter for the Chahtas to raise a sufficient force to cross the river and scalp every man, woman and child in three days. The people were greatly alarmed, and though there was no real ground for it, besides the stories the boatmen had told on their return about the thousands of Indians they had seen and shot at in the prairie, the account had been bandied from mouth to mouth until it had grown into frightful dimensions. Some were talking of gathering up some of their available things, and getting away from the dangerous country as soon as possible. Others were urging the necessity of arming and meeting the Indians in battle. They were hooted at. All were seriously alarmed and no plan that could be offered seemed to suit the emergency.

The chief, Mushulatubi, who had heard that my wife had become frightened at my absence, not knowing what had become of me, and the terrible scalping stories that had been sent over to her, had gone over to town, got some awkward pensman amongst his workmen to write her a letter, telling her not to be frightened, that let what would happen, no Chahta was base enough to injure her, or anything belonging to her. This badly indicted letter was passed from hand to hand and interpreted into as many meanings. All agreed however that it was an ominous letter and meant a great deal; that it contained concealed intimations and they were certain that it was in some way connected with my unaccountable absence. Plain enough. And as soon as I should come back, if I ever did, I must give a satisfactory explanation, or—they did not say what they would do with me.

In the height of this panic and great trepidation I made my appearance. I could not imagine what was the matter with the people. I was instantly surrounded, and was asked a thousand questions in a minute. Where have you been? What have you been after? How many Indians are embodied over the river, etc., etc., until in my amazement, I told them all to go to—somewhere.

As soon as I could disenthrall myself from the eagerly inquiring crowd, I went to the magistrate's office, told him what I had done, and delivered the bond I had taken from Atoba, for his appearance at the time specified in the bond. After he had examined it he said it was satisfactory; and a good deal better way than to arrest him and hold him in prison until the next court. Nevertheless, some of the knowing ones after the subsidence of the panic, mouthed a good deal about the manner in which the thing had been conducted, and accused their magistrate of having been bribed.

Time passed quickly, and the day for the trial came. As early as ten A.M. the white people from Columbus had collected at the oak grove in great numbers. It was a beautiful day; the people were lounging in various groups under the shady oaks, seeming to be quite agreeably situated. Having plenty of good water near by, there was nothing to mar the good feelings inspired by the pleasant grove and fine day, except the presence of forty head of marauding, half-intoxicated boatmen and their drunken associates. They had their bottles hidden out, and they were "browsing" about in the surrounding thickets like so many brutes, as they were.

The balance of the assembly was civil enough, but no Indians had arrived yet, and the white people were becoming restless. It was in vain that they were told that the hour specified in the bond was twelve o'clock and that it lacked over an hour of that time. They sneeringly replied that it was a sell, and good enough, as they might have had better sense than to think that Atoba, or any one else, would be fool enough to make his appearance, after being set at liberty in the foolish manner he had and for such a crime.

Fifteen minutes of twelve, and no sign of Indians yet. The crowd had become painfully impatient. Some of them were talking about starting back to town and swearing that they never had been so completely entrapped in all their lives. Some were hungry, and others wanted their customary "horn of brandy." They were in a woeful fix. But twelve o'clock would come in spite of their doubts and impatience; and with the meridian sun, the prisoner, accompanied by about three hundred other Indians, all mounted and well armed. Among them were the three chiefs of the nation. They made their approach in single file, observing good order. It was a long string of warriors, making quite a formidable appearance. Atoba was not armed, and he occupied a position near the center of the line; and he looked ashamed and not dissatisfied. They came briskly up right into the grove of oaks, all amongst the scattered groups of unarmed white men.

I looked around on the then silenced assembly; the vociferous clamor about the faithless Indians biting hunger and want of liquor was all hushed. And I thought I saw a good many pale faces.

The Indians, however, broke ranks, went to the bushes and little trees that skirted the grove, and, after hitching their horses, set their guns against the trees and in their usually friendly manner mixed into the crowd of white people, shaking hands with all they met; and at the same time ejaculating their various terms used by them, at their friendly greeting. And then the white folks began to smile too.

A table and some benches had been provided and there were seated around the table five justices of the peace, and as many lawyers. Among the lawyers was the venerable William Cocke. Atoba came and took his seat as near to the table as he could get, and said "I am here."

The court organized, and the examination of the case commenced.

The chiefs, Mushulatubi, Apukshinubi and Apushimataha, were invited to take seats among the magistrates, which they did, and seemed to be pleased at it, and to regard it as a proper token of respect. The examination of the witnesses then followed. There were about twenty-five witnesses, mostly women. I was one, and was called and qualified first. My testimony was the same as I have already stated while describing the circumstances connected with the killing and need not be repeated. The next witness was a Chickasa woman. She manifested signs of considerable embarrassment, but when the nature and penalty of the oath had been explained to her she "blowed the book," and in good style delivered herself, word for word, as she had told me at the window, the same night the man was killed. The balance of the female witnesses, about fifteen, who were seated on a stock of hewn timber near the store at the time the accident occurred, were sworn, one at a time, and they repeated what the Chickasa woman had testified to almost *verbatim*. All the

testimony went to show very clearly that the killing was accidental, and that Atoba was not only innocent, but that he was particularly friendly to the man he had in his drunkenness unfortunately
killed.

As soon as the boatmen and rowdies who were on the council
grounds discovered that no criminality could be established against
Atoba and that he would be acquitted, they collected in squads
about and were trying to get up an excitement for the purpose of
mobbing the Indians, and perhaps the council of majesty and lawyers "into the bargain." Some Chahtas who understood English
overheard their plottings and went and informed Apushimataha of
it. Apushimataha, who had satisfied himself that the trial was conducted fairly, had left the table, and when the Indian that brought
the news of the contemplated riot came to him he was seated a little
way off from the crowd, on the fence. After hearing what the Indians had to say about the plot he slid down from the fence, went
directly to the council, took up a book, and stamping it on the table,
said:

> It is to you, my white brothers, that I wish to address myself this
> fair day. I had kept my seat among the wise and good men who were
> conducting the investigation of my friend Atoba's case until I satis-
> fied myself that the trial is a fair one; and I had, as there was no
> further use for my presence, gone off a little way, and was seated in
> a pleasant place, amusing myself with the contemplation of the mag-
> nitude of the government and wonderful greatness of the American
> people, when one of my own countrymen came and informed me
> that a number of white men, now present (for when Apushimataha
> went to the table they had gathered around to hear him speak), who
> have no families or anything else that is valuable in the country to
> detain them when they are guilty of an outrage, are counseling
> among one another; and their aim is to break up the peace and
> friendly intercourse that has always obtained between the Chahtas
> and the American white people. It must be prevented. It will be put
> a stop to——

At this point the venerable William Cocke, who was familiarly acquainted with the speaker, interrupted him and remarked, "Brother

Push, you speak too bold and plain; it might occasion the spilling of blood." Apushimataha listened but made no reply at that time. He, however, continued and said:

> I would have you, my white brothers, to understand that I have visited the big white house where our father, the President, resides; and locking my five fingers with his five fingers we made a treaty of peace, in the presence of that Being under the shadow of whose far spreading wings we all exist, whose strong arm extends through all orders of the animal creation and down into the lowest grass and herbs in the forest. It was in the presence of this *shilombish*—spirit— that we made our peace, swept our paths clean, made them white; and on my part, and I speak for the entire Chahta people, there has been no track made in them. If, after a fair investigation, this unfortunate man, Atoba, shall be found guilty, we will give him up, cheerfully submit him to his destiny. We came here determined to do that. But on the other hand, if he is not found guilty, we shall sustain him like men, and we will do it at all hazards. I here frankly confess that I feel no misgivings in relation to the wise and very respectable gentlemen who are managing the trial. I know them all personally; I am satisfied with them, and shall yield to their decision in the case. But it is to the reckless, loose crowd of irresponsible men to whom I have made allusion; men who are here to-day and there tomorrow; men who care no more for the white man than he does for the red man, and who would be willing sacrifice both for a frolic with a big jug of whisky. These are the kind of men I speak of. They are here close by; they hear my voice now; and when they have matured their plot and make the attempt to put it into action, if the officers of this well conducted council desire that it shall be suppressed, and are not in sufficient force to accomplish it, let them call on me and I will instantly bring to their aid at a single whoop all the Chahtas who are on the ground. If the court do not see fit to call the red people to their assistance, and suffer a riot to occur here to-day, I shall take it upon myself to assume the responsibility in suppressing any outrage that may be attempted in this Chahta grove of red oaks, either while the council holds its session or after they have adjourned.

Then turning to the venerable Judge Cocke, he said, "Konka nokni sipokni" (old chicken cock, the name he was known by among the Chahtas), "Speak not to me of blood. I was raised in blood." He then very quietly seated himself on the bench near the old judge.

The above speech was interpreted into English by John Pitchlynn, who had been United States interpreter for the Chahta nation ever since the Hopewell treaty. The rowdy boatsmen were all jammed up as near as they could get, and heard every word, for Pitchlynn rendered it in good English, and spoke quite loud and distinct. Apushimataha's manner and the bold tone of his voice while speaking had subdued their malicious intentions and they were all perfectly dumb. They looked at each other and said nothing, but when they turned their eyes, which had been riveted upon Apushimataha while he was delivering his little speech, and discovered that the Indians' guns, which had been all day leaning against the trees, were all gone, they became alarmed, and as it was getting late in the day, they excused themselves and departed for Columbus.

The examination of the testimony was concluded, and after some short speeches by two or three of the lawyers, Atoba was acquitted. But he was not satisfied, and in the course of a month he was found drowned in the river.

With all his greatness, no one knew or could tell anything about the origin of parentage of Apushimataha. And this was a secret of which he seemed to be very proud. I made efforts often, among the people of his district when they came about me, trying to find some scraps of items in relation to the history of his early life. It was an entire failure. I saw no one that knew anything about him until he was about eighteen or nineteen years of age. John Pitchlynn, who was a few years older than Apushimataha, was raised in the nation from his fourth year. He was as ignorant of the early history of the great chief as everybody else, although he had, and he told me of it himself, sought long and in various ways to unriddle the perplexing secret.

The first notice of Apushimataha that anybody could tell was in a hunting party. It was a bear hunt. And when the party had camped the first night on their journey to the hunting ground, it was observed that there was a lean, meager-looking lad in the camps that seemed to be a stranger. There were no remarks made about it, for the hunting party was quite large, numbering over a hundred men, and had it not been for his peculiar lean and rather haggard appearance he perhaps would not have attracted attention at all, for in so large a company it was to be expected that there would be some strangers. It was, however, after a day or two, discovered that the lad was unknown to the whole party, and was becoming the subject of inquiry throughout the camps. Who is the bony, badly-clad stripling? Was in everybody's mouth. No one knew who he was or where he came from. To ask a stranger for his name is great impoliteness in Chahta etiquette; and now the strange lad had created so much curiosity amongst them that they could no longer contain themselves, and so they put it upon the oldest man to go and have a talk with him and find out from whence he came and his name. When the man came back to his comrades from the talk he held with the young man he reported that when he asked him from what land he came he replied, "luma" (obscure, hidden), and to the inquiry for his name he answered, "hohchifoiksho" (nameless). These answers only served to excite a greater degree of curiosity; but as he was deporting himself very civilly and was quietly bearing his part in the duties about the camps of nights they did not feel warranted in pushing the inquiry further, and so contented themselves by calling him by the name he had given, "Hohchifiolsho," until some circumstance should turn up that would unfold the mystery or enable them to give him an appropriate name.

They at length reached the country they had designated for the winter's hunt; the weather was fine, the hunters all hungry; and they did not stop to prepare camps, but concluded to go immediately into the hunt for the purpose of procuring some fresh bear meat to begin with. In those days there were but few guns among the Chahtas, and at least half the party in the present hunt were armed with bow and arrows. The nameless lad from the obscure country had a good knife and bow and arrows only. But it was observed that his arrows were of the very best pattern and his bow was a strong one. The wonder was how he could manage to shoot such a bow, and when they were about to leave the camps, going to the hunt, they signified to the bony young man that he would do better to remain in camps, as he seemed not to be in good health, and as the hunt would continue three or four moons, he would have plenty of hunting opportunities after he got well. He told them calmly, but firmly, that he came to hunt and not to keep camp. They said no more, but all went off into the bear hunt. It was early morning when they started and they had a hard day's hunt of it. They killed a good many bears, and had, when they brought into camp their rich supply of fat meat at night, many incidents, some dangerous and some funny, that had occurred during the day, all highly interesting to the bear hunter. There were a few instances of very narrow escape from being crushed by a terrible hug and from being chewed to pieces by the irresistible teeth of the wounded bears. But the most daring feat that took place in that day's hunt was perpetrated by the nameless lad, and it was said and oft repeated, while they were regaling themselves with their greasy supper, that he had made the most wonderful escape. He told them that what he had done that day was nothing in comparison to what he could and would perform before they got through with the hunt. The other hunters hearing what he said he would do before the hunt was over said "that's good, and he is now entitled to a name by which we can hereafter call him. He shall bear the name of 'Ishtilauata'" (to brag or boast). And so they called him this until he procured a higher title by subsequent daring.

Sure enough "Ishtilauata," as they now called the nameless lad, performed the most daring and seemingly reckless feats of any of the men in the hunt. It occurred not once in a while, but every day; and he killed and preserved a greater amount of meat and more skins than any one hunter, even the most experienced among them.

The winter's hunt turned out to be a successful one, and spring returning brought the time for packing their dry meats and pelfry to their distant homes. A party of the hunters numbering about forty warriors, who were desirous of having something to talk about when they got home, concluded to cross the Mississippi, for it was in the extensive canebrake bottoms of that great river that they had made their hunt, and pay a visit to the Ovashsashi nation for the purpose of taking a few scalps so as to have a war dance when they returned to their own nation. When the leader "beat up" for volunteers to constitute a war party Ishtilauata was the first that stepped out. A good many of those who did not intend to join the war party seeing "brag" the first one to respond to the call of the leader, burst into an uproarous laugh and prophesied that the expedition would turn out unsuccessful. "Brag" cast contemptuous looks at them but made no remarks.

The party was soon made up, and while they were making arrangements with those who remained behind to get their meat home Ishtilauata went to some of the hunters who were rather old and who had not been very successful in the hunt and gave them his hunt, meat, skins and all, telling them at the same time that he had no home or relatives of any kind, and if they would divide his hunt equally amongst them they should be welcome to it. They were greatly pleased with the unexpected liberality of the young hunter, and for the great favor expressed many thanks.

The party were soon ready and made a cheerful start on their perilous enterprise. They crossed the Mississippi on dry cane rafts and pursued their journey for many days. Coming at length to the great prairies where roamed the Ovashsashi people, the leader halted and, concealing the party in a dense hammock of timber and thick undergrowth, sent out one or two spies to ascertain if any camps were in the vicinity and also, if they found no encampment, to notice and select a good hiding place further on, and they would cross the prairies to it by night.

After two days the spies returned and reported that they had discovered no encampments or any fresh signs. On a river about half a day's travel, right ahead, there was a very good place for concealment and a chance to procure some provisions about the river and its thick bottoms. They set out across the prairie as soon as it was dark, and reaching the river bottom some time before day concealed themselves securely, remaining there all the next day. In the meantime, however, they had sent spies with instructions not to go very far, but to make a very close examination for signs, and as they were now in the enemy's country, they must be exceedingly cautious and not make any signs themselves. The Ovashsashis, said the leader, are a wonderfully sagacious people, and would notice the slightest signs. They know the natural position of every leaf and blade of grass, and fail not, when they discover a blade of grass or leaf of the trees turned in an unnatural position, or a stick that had been moved from its bed since the last rain, to stop and examine it until they had satisfied themselves how it had happened to be so placed. Therefore, the spies were charged to leave no signs on the line of their travel of any kind. For should the presence of the Chahtas war party be discovered by that kind of carelessness the consequence would be disastrous, and for it there would be no remedy or possibility of escape.

When the spies came into camp they reported that they had discovered a considerable party on the plains, whom they had at first supposed to be a war party. They had, however, trailed them all day, and found at night that they went to their camps, and then they discovered by the scaffolds of meat and women and children at the camp that they were a hunting party. They could not venture near enough to ascertain any thing in regard to their numbers, but it was a large encampment, and they entertained the opinion that they were quite numerous. The leader of the Chahta party then held a war talk, at which it was decided to make a night attack on their camps. The programme of the attack was to approach the camp from three sides of it and if the party should be too strong for them and force them to retreat the Chahta warriors must disperse and, scattering in all directions, reassemble at the place of concealment on the river as soon as possible.

They arrived in sight of the Ovashsashi camp fires about midnight, and dividing themselves into three parties, approached the camp from three directions, as had been previously arranged, and by a preconcerted signal the onset commenced a little after midnight. Soon the uproar was very great. The Chahta warriors silenced a great many of them, but their numbers were so great that as soon as they had recovered themselves a little they rallied rapidly to a signal whoop that was made a little off to one side of the camp. Seeing that they were an overpowering host of warriors the Chahtas discharged a volley of arrows and what guns they had amongst the gathering Ovashsashis, and hastily scattered themselves over the plains, every man taking his own direction.

By the middle of the next night the entire party had reached the hiding place except the young man that they called "Brag." The conclusion was that he had been scalped at the camp, or had exposed himself and had been overtaken by a war party during the day. They lay close all the next day, only peeping out occasionally from the borders of the thick brush that concealed and protected them from the ferocious and highly excited warriors of the Ovashsashi people. Notwithstanding the fact that the Chahtas had slain quite a number of the camp of the Ovashsashis, on account of their hasty and precipitate retreat, they had taken but one scalp. They had not time to take more. This was by them considered a great misfortune, over which they grieved.

Early after dark the ensuing night they left their hiding place, and as they knew the whole Ovashsashi nation would soon be out on the hunt for them, they concluded to make their way, as best they could, towards their own country, and for that purpose set out to cross the prairie and reach, if possible, the thick hammock in which they had concealed themselves the first time. They were silently passing over the wide plain, and when about the middle of it found themselves suddenly surrounded by a large party of loudly yelling warriors. They formed themselves into a close column and essayed to continue their way. Ovashsashis pressed so heavily upon their front and yelled so incessantly that the Chahtas could plainly perceive that they were in sufficient force to cut off their retreat. The darkness of the night prevented both parties from attempting a charge, or from wasting their missiles by shooting, when they could only distinguish the objects as moving shadows on the prairie. The Chahtas parlied, and swaying about on the deep sea of prairie grass, they accidentally came across and fell into a considerable lime sink, that terminated at the bottom in an underground passage of some extent, sufficient to receive and conceal the entire party. Here they took refuge. In the bottom of the little cave was a small rill of running water, and they could, by jamming closely together, retire so far back into the little cavern that they were out of reach of the missiles from above. They had a little cold flour and a few scraps of dry meat. On making an equal partition of their provision stores they came to the conclusions that they would be able to hold out ten days. All had become quiet above. The leader cautiously peeped out, but could make no discoveries, only that it was still dark. The night had not passed away, and they knew that the Ovashsashi warriors, wolflike, were watching patiently for their prey. At length the day began to creep into the mouth of the little cavern, and they could not hear the slightest sounds of any description. They knew that it would not do for them to look out for a single moment. The profound silence was ominous of an attack, perfectly understood by the Chahtas, and they made preparation with all the means they possessed to receive the onset of the numerous foe in as good style as their crowded position would allow. The plan was for those who had rifles to stand in front, nearest to the mouth of the cave, and to fire their piece only when the mark was a sure one. And finally, if the enemy should attempt to storm the cave, their knives were to be resorted to and applied in the most desperate manner. The sun had been up some time and his golden rays had begun to glance down the western declivity of the lime sink, which formed the entrance to the cavern. No voice had come from above yet. All inside the cavern was still as death.

Presently a terrific yell of numerous voices broke forth and instantly large quantities of grass, weeds and various other combustible materials were let fall from above, immediately in the mouth of the cave. Incessantly the combustibles were tumbling down, from which the Chahtas knew that the intention of the Ovashsashis was to burn them up, or at least to suffocate them with smoke. The Chahtas drew into the cave all the grass and weeds that fell in reach of them, and wetting them in the little stream of water that dribbled through the bottom of the cave, began to form a wet barricade across the mouth of it. While they were thus employed an arrow came in, narrowly missing the man who was at that moment packing down the wet weeds at the mouth of the cave. The Chahta leader, then taking advantage of the pile of weeds which was piled up for a defense against the fire and smoke, peeped out and could distinctly see the head of a man peering over the farther bank of the lime sink. To a person outside it was all dark in the cave, and the motion

of the leader not being perceived he took deadly aim at the head of
the Ovashsashi, and firing his rifle "centered" his forehead. In the
death scuffle the Ovashsashi rolled down into the bottom of the
lime sink. And now the uproar above was terrific beyond description, and great numbers of the enraged Ovashsashis rushed down
to the dead man, attempting at the same time to storm the cave.
The Chahtas kept up such a deadly fire on them they were compelled
to retreat, carrying off with them several other dead men. For a few
minutes they remained silent. Then again the war whoop resounded,
seemingly from a great multitude. The Chahtas had time while the
war whoop was going on to fix up their arrangements a little and
to resolve amongst themselves to sell their lives as dearly as possible.

Soon again the combustibles were tumbling down in larger quantities than before. The Chahtas could see very distinctly that their
fate was sealed, and their greatest desire now was to kill as many of
the howling foe as they could. They had cut out, with their knives
and pipe hatchets, niches in the sides of the cave, that secured them
from the arrows of the enemy, and from which they could fight
better with their knives in case the enemy should succeed in getting
in. They had also succeeded in stopping one side of the mouth of
the cave nearly to the top with wet grass and weeds, which they had
snatched in at the moment the bundles were falling. The leader now
having a secure hiding place, kept up a vigilant lookout, hoping to
get a shot at another head.

It was not long, however, until the lime sink was so far filled up
that they could get as much as they wanted of the materials they
were throwing down and they packed the mouth of the cavern with
a thick wall of it, which they made wet by constantly throwing what
water they could get upon it. All within now was utter darkness.
And they were silently waiting in a very hopeless condition. They
were not, however, permitted to brood over their misfortunes a great
while before they heard the crackling flames, which soon increased
to a terrific roar.

The combustibles had been lightly thrown in and they were soon
consumed. The heat was sufficiently intense to convert the water
that had been thrown on the grass in the mouth of the cave into

steam, which soon filled the cavern and was very annoying, but after the grass had become partially dry, it also took fire and soon filled the cave with suffocating smoke. This was terrible and the dampened grass burnt so slow that it seemed that the smoke would have no end to it. The smoke was so intensely severe that had it not been for the water in the cave the whole party must have died. As it was, they did not lack much of being smoked to death.

At last the grass was all consumed, and contrary to all expectations, there was no attack made upon the cave, neither could any noises be heard. They peeped out all they could, but could make no discoveries. Night came, and though they held their ears against the walls of the cave, they could hear no sounds of any kind. The supposition was that the Ovashsashis were lying in wait for them, and no one would dare go out. After midnight one of the Chahtas who had been asleep said the enemy were gone. In a dream he had seen them trotting across the prairie like a gang of wild turkeys. So strong was he impressed with the belief that the Ovashsashis were gone he could not be prevailed on to lie still, but would creep out and look. After some time he returned and reported that they were sure enough all gone. He said he had encircled the place to a considerable distance and that they were most certainly gone. He noticed that the grass had been clean burnt from the prairie and was still burning all around at the distance of a mile or two. By laying his head low on the ground and lighting the surface by the blaze of the burning grass he could very distinctly see that there were no moving things or any lumps or masses of any kind that he did not understand. It was quite calm, and there was nothing to be seen between himself and the fire excepting the thousands of white wreaths of smoke, which were shooting upwards in all directions from the slowly smoldering buffalo chips.

It was an unaccountable mystery, but it was true that when they had all cautiously come out from the cave there was no indication of an enemy anywhere to be seen or heard. There was no time to parley about it, and so made arrangements to meet in the far off hammock of thick woods.

All got in safe before sunrise, and concealing themselves stealthily, they slept the greater portion of the day, except the watchers. The hammock was a little elevated, and by climbing some of the tall, leafy trees, they could overlook the burning plains for a day's journey. They could see no Ovashsashis.

What had become of them no one could conjecture. It forced the Chahtas to observe extreme cautiousness and when the night came again they silently set out on their journey homeward. For fear that the mysterious disappearance of the Ovashsashis was a strategic movement to draw them from the cave and to entrap them in an ambuscade, the Chahtas placed themselves in a very singular marching order. They marched in single file and as far apart as they could see one another, so that if they should stumble into an ambuscade there would be but three or four in it at any one time. In this manner they traveled all night. Nothing turned up to annoy them and they spent the next day in the thick bottom of a little creek.

Having time now to breathe a little freer some of the party spied round a little, while others slept or employed themselves "raking" the creek for something to eat. The whole party had escaped with the exception of Ishtilauata. They had not seen him since the attack on the Ovashsashi camp, and the supposition was that he had been killed, or as he was an unknown straggler, not caring much where he was and besides not having been kindly treated during the expedition, it would not be a very strange thing, under all the circumstances, to hear some day hence that the ill-treated young man had gone over to the Ovashsashi people. All could see, now it was too late, that they had been unkind to him, for they said he was a truthful young man.

Night was approaching and they were fixing up their packs for the journey, when just about twilight Ishtilauata came quietly up and took a seat near the crowd, who were engaged in planning the manner of the travel through the night. All saw him at once, and with evident signs of unfeigned gladness the whole party exclaimed:

"Hallo, 'Brag;' why, where did you come from? We had just been talking about you, and our former conclusions were that if you were not dead you had joined the Ovashsashi people."

"In reference to me you often make mistakes. I am neither dead nor turned Ovashsashi, as you see," he very calmly replied.

"Well, well, 'Brag,' don't be offended at us; we were all sorry and had confessed among ourselves that we had not behaved toward you with as much respect as you really do merit."

"That," said he, "is because you don't know me; but the day will come when you shall all know me. You call me 'Ishtilauati' now. I shall return that name upon the head of those who gave it, and they shall brag then, not of their own deeds of daring, but of mine."

"Come, 'Brag,' don't be ill any longer, but tell where you were in time of the fight at the Ovashsashi camp."

"I stayed among the warriors, where the fighting was going on, what little there was of it," he replied.

"Yes, you stayed with the warriors," they sarcastically remarked.

Ishtilauata quickly replied, "Why dispute my word, when you know you were not there to see me?"

"Oh, then, you were a prisoner and have made shift to escape?"

"I was no prisoner," said Ishtilauata, "but I was where I could see the Ovashsashi warriors piling and burning grass and weeds in a cave upon those who were."

"You, somehow or other, have been fortunate. We will ask no more questions, but beg of you to be so kind as to give us a history of your mysterious adventure."

Ishtilauata good humoredly remarked: "I will do that, as it will save you a good deal of guessing; and I will also clear up another mystery to you, which you have no means of accounting for, and that hangs heavier on your minds than did the uneasiness experienced on account of my absence."

"Well, say on," they all anxiously urged, and as you speak so much like an old, experienced warrior, we will all hear you and give credit to all you tell us."

"That's all very well," said Ishtilauata, "but if your incredulity should overpower and prevent you from having full faith in what I shall narrate to you, I shall be able to force conviction by producing the evidence. But," continued he, "we must travel to-night, and as my story is a long one and will be of no advantage under the circumstances for you to know it now, I must postpone its revealment until we reach a situation of greater security."

They took up the line of march, making a long journey, part of which lay along the border of a river bottom, which they turned into for concealment on the approach of the morning light. Their provisions were all out, and necessity compelled them, after a short sleep, to look around for something to eat. Five of the party went over to the highlands as spies. They returned by the middle of the day and reported that they had seen no signs of a recent date, and from what discoveries they could make on the locality, gave it as their opinion that they had passed the bounds of the Ovashsashi country.

Some of them went hunting in the bottom and found some deer, a few of which they killed with their bows. None but bowmen were allowed to go in the hunt, for fear of being discovered. But while the bowmen were packing up some deer they had killed, they were startled by the firing of five or six guns at the camp, and supposing that the Ovashsashi had found them, they left their meat and ran with great haste to the camp. When they came near they "parlied" to listen, and were much gratified to hear their own men talking and laughing. They then approached the camp and found that the firing had been occasioned by three fine bear that had attempted to pass where the men were laying resting. They succeeded in taking all three of the bear, which, with the venison they had, made a plentiful supply of meat for a day or two.

After a plentiful feast they unanimously called on Ishtilauata to narrate his adventure, and also to give the promised explanation of the mysterious manner in which the Ovashsashis had fled when they left the burning cave.

He began his narrative at the Ovashsashi camp and said that when the Chahtas were from superior numbers forced to retreat he was a little ways apart from the main body scalping a man that he had transfixed with an arrow, and that the retreat was so precipitate that he found himself instantly left alone; Ovashsashi and all passed on in the flight, and the pursuit giving him time to go and scalp another man that he saw fall at the first onset. Soon he began to hear voices and he slipped off to the left of the course the rout had taken and hiding in some rank weeds he had in the dark stumbled into, remained there until the uproar of the pursuit was over and the Ovashsashis had all returned to their camp. He then glided off and shaping his course for the thick hammock they had camped in the day previous to the attack made what speed he could until daybreak, where, being in the thick brushwood of the river bottom, he crawled into concealment and remained undisturbed through the day. As soon as it was dark he set out again, crossed the river and was traveling in the prairie when he heard the shouting of the Ovashsashis far off to his right. He knew what it meant and hurried onward, turning his course more and more to the right until he was as he judged two miles or more beyond where the conflict was going on. By the time he found some rank weed and grass to hide in all had become silent, and being greatly exhausted he fell asleep and remained unconscious of the world's action until sunup, when he was aroused from his refreshing sleep by the terrific war whoop. He carefully peeped out from his grassy concealment from whence he could distinctly see the entire Ovashsashi force. They were nearer to him than he liked, but there was no chance for him to change his position now. There was no timber in sight in the direction he wished to go, nothing but a continued plain of short grass, not high enough to hide a turkey except in the occasional patches of half grown weeds. He kept his place, saw them throwing into the cave grass and weed in great quantities. Heard the sharp crack of the rifle and saw the man who was shot tumble over the brink of the lime sink. Then went up the war whoop, more terrific than before, followed by a charge of the whole force. Many men went down out of sight in to the lime sink. He heard more guns, and soon they came out again, dragging back with them four dead men. Over this pile of dead warriors they held a short parley, when a party of their warriors brought the dead more than half way to his place of concealment, and, laying them down in the grass, returned, carrying turns of combustibles to the cave. For a considerable length of time the whole party were energetically engaged in filling up the lime sink with everything they could get that would burn. They then set fire to it, and for a while the cloud of white smoke that went up from it was wonderful. It went up in the form of a large white cloud to the very sky; it was a calm day and it mounted upwards on nearly a straight line and was doubtless visible for a day's journey around. Then it kindled into a flame, roaring like a storm. And while their warriors were dancing and exulting over their burning victims he saw another larger party of warriors coming from towards the river timber, running very rapidly. He supposed them to be a party of the same people who had seen the great cloud of smoke and were coming from towards the river timber, running very rapidly, to their assistance. He gave up all as lost and was thinking of the folly of a handful of Chahtas making war upon such a powerful nation of warriors who were as swift on foot as the deer and ferocious as the long clawed bear, and was weeping at the dreadful fate of his companions when he observed a sudden wild stir among the straw-gathering Ovashsashis. It seemed to be a perfect panic. The war whoop ceased and they dropped the grass they were carrying and flying to and gathering their scattered implements of war they fled away over the prairie very rapidly. But they were pursued by men of swifter foot who passed, not far from his place of concealment, sweeping over the grassy plain like the fierce *apeli* (hurricane). He could not count them but supposed them to be about four hundred and fifty or perhaps five hundred. Who they were or to what nation they belonged he possessed no means of finding out. They were armed with short bows and full quivers of arrows, but they passed without uttering a single word or vocal sound of any kind. They were tall, well formed, looking as much alike as the deer. The Ovashsashis whom he had counted two or three times numbered two hundred and eighty-four. But if their numbers had been equal they would have been no match for the pursuing tribe. He could see that they were gaining ground on the Ovashsashi, but they soon faded away from his vision as they fled into the increasing vapor of the far-reaching plain westwardly. The day was far spent and turning his eyes toward the cave he saw that the old dry grass had taken fire, which being very dry was sufficient in quantity to consume the new growth, and it was crackling and slowly widening around the cave its blackened area. The combustibles that had been thrown into the lime sink had burnt out and there were only a few curling wreaths of blue smoke coming up from the smouldering embers.

"'Well' said I, talking to myself, 'I am left alone in this dreary endless plain. My friends were all consumed in the lime sink and my enemies have been chased away by a people unknown to me. I need not go to the lime sink to see about the fate of my companions. There could be no possible chance for them to survive so great a fire, and alone as I am I could do nothing with so many dead bodies. When it is night, however, I will go and take the hair of the dead warriors I saw the Ovashsashis deposit in the grass, and that being half way to the cave, I will pass near the cave and call the names of my suffocated friends one by one, and that must satisfy their wandering *shilup* as far as I am concerned.' Thus soliloquizing, I waited for the coming night. The dullness and stillness of twilight in that lifeless desert hung heavily on my senses, and dropping to sleep did not wake until the evening was far spent. It must have been hear the middle of the night. I was hungry and thirsty, and as the nearest water was the river I had crossed the night before, I was at a loss to know how to proceed. Revenge prompted me, and I decided to have the scalps of the warriors. While I was at the place where they lay I thought I heard somebody spit, and looking around saw two men, one on either side of me, walking pretty fast. They were too far off for me to see anything but that they were men. I, of course, instantly dropped in the grass. They passed quickly, making no more noise, and as I could not hear their footfalls, I concluded that, if there be any *shilup*, I had seen two of them. After scalping the stiffened warriors, I examined around to see if I could find anything to eat, finding a small sack of something I supposed to be eatables and a scrap of grizzled buffalo meat, which I eagerly put into my mouth, and hurried round by the cave to ascertain if possible the fate of my unfortunate companions. Coming to the brink of the lime sink, I could discern a dark section on the opposite side, which I took to be a hole. After due caution, I descended and found it to be what I had thought it to be. I spoke low several times, but receiving no answer I ventured to enter. Soon the whole matter was explained to me, and helping myself to what I needed of the bountiful supply of good water I found in the bottom of the little cavern, I was rejoiced to know by the empty cave that my companions had all escaped. I had kept watch over it ever since the Ovashsashis had been chased away, and knowing that they had not returned could understand to my full satisfaction that my friends had left the cave and were safe somewhere. With a light heart I set out on the route towards home, traveling as fast as I could till near sunup, when I concealed myself in a clump of small bushes and slept the greater portion of the day. As soon as it was dark I moved forward again, when at daybreak I found myself on the border of the swamp and not far from the place where you were camped. I went a little way into the thick swamp and while lying there I heard voices which I soon recognized as my own comrades. They passed very near where I lay, but did not see me. I trailed them until I found where you were camped, when I lay down again, waiting until you were making preparations to go forward, when, as you all remember, I came and sat down amongst you. I was greatly rejoiced to find the whole party safe."

"Your talk, Istilauata, is a good one and very well spoken. You have narrated some wonderful events and mysterious occurrences, such as never happened to anyone before; but at the beginning you promised to clear up the doubtful part of your adventure by producing the testimony, and you must not think hard of us when we tell you that our incredulity has been so heavily taxed by your wonderful accounts of the war feats and extremely well conducted management in evading the enemy, in finding your company, after examining the cave where they had been burnt alive, which you witnessed, besides your success in killing one man, which you scalped, with five other cases of scalping, which you did not say you killed, if we require of you to produce the testimony."

"I am," said the strippling Ishtilauata, "fully able to satisfy you. In the first place, I must bring to your minds the fact that you parted from me on the night of the attack on the Ovashsashi camp and that I am now here with you safe and sound. That I saw the Ovashsashi warriors burning you in the lime sink you cannot deny, for I have described the manner in which they accomplished it. That I saw a large body of warriors of some, to me, unknown people chase the Ovashsashis away from the burning cave you must take for the truth, inasmuch as you have no other way to account for their mysterious disappearance. That I went into and examined the cave you will know is true or false when I tell you that I found running water there and drank of it. That I killed and scalped a warrior at the Ovashsashi camp you will be able to understand from the bloody feathers on this arrow, which I drew out by the point, and also by this lock of hair and skin. That I scalped another warrior who had been killed by I know not whom you must decide by the examination of that war lock of hair. That I scalped the four warriors who were killed by somebody at the time they made their charge on the cave you must take these four scalps as testimony; and that I profited by finding where the Ovashsashis laid their dead warriors you will discover when you examine this little leather bag of pounded venison, these two good arrows and this powerful bow."

All of these he unfolded, while he was speaking, from a long roll which he had been carrying in his pack.

The whole party confessed their astonishment when they could no longer doubt the truth of his report. His wonderful management and singular success drew forth expressions of praise and admiration from all the warriors present, and it was proposed that he should have a big war name bestowed on him. He, however, calmly, but firmly, refused, at the same time remarking that when he consented to receive a war name it must be for something more than one scalp of his own killing or for an adventure he might tell of himself. A war name for him to accept must be predicated on deeds of great daring which must be seen and told by other men. "You believe," he added, "what I have told you, and it is most certainly true; but what account would a war name be at home based upon my individual say so, supported by the testimony only of a defeated party? No, no; give me no war name for what has accidentally occurred to me this time."

No one offered any further proposition, all looking upon his strippling form with wonder and admiration. The leader of the party remarked that he was a strange kind of young man and possessed wisdom beyond his years. He declared that the lad spoke like an experienced chief and predicted that some day or other he was destined to lead the nation.

They returned home without any further adventure, had a big war dance which Ishtilauata, who had previously placed all the scalps in the hands of the leader, did not attend. Everybody wondered at his absenting himself from such an occasion; but the leader told the people that it was just like him, that he was a peculiar young man who did not seek honors; and as for himself he said he had not expected him at the war dance at all. The war party had nobody else but Istilauata to talk about, and as he was known to no one who participated at the dance the question was often asked, "Who is he?

Where did he come from?" To what iksa does he belong?" etc. But no one could tell, and they were greatly perplexed. No one knew where he went or what had become of him even then. And they made use of all the means they possessed to trace him. It all failed, and had it not been for the testimony of the hunters the war party had left behind when they crossed the Mississippi people would have maintained that the wonderful accounts of his great war feats was all fiction and that there was no such person. The talk soon ended amongst the people, and we hear no more of Ishtilauata until he turns up a year or two later at a great battle which took place between the Chahtas and Muskogies on the Tuscaloosa River not far below where the town of Tuscaloosa, Alabama, now stands.

The Muskogees and Chahtas had been long at war about the ownership of the district of country lying between the Black Warrior rivers. The dispute was not settled until the Muskogees were conquered by Gen. A. Jackson in 1814. Consequently the Chahtas and Muskogees had very many battles, which war had continued many years previous to the battle of Tuscaloosa at which Ishtilauata made his next appearance after the war dance over the Ovashsashi scalps. He came with no party of warriors, nor had he been noted by any of the war parties until the battle had been going on for some time. The Muskogees had met and given battle to the Chahtas on the west side of the river below their town, which was on the east side. The battle was a hard one, the Muskogees fighting under cover of an immense canebrake and the Chahtas from behind the bark trees, and the declivity of the rising ground. At length, about the center of the line of battle, there was a charge made by a small party of Chahtas upon the Muskogee warriors. The Muskogees gave way, and at that moment a shout of victory went up from the little party which brought on a general charge, and the Muskogees fled wildly to the river where numbers of them were killed while they were crossing it.

Night closing in prevented the further progress of the battle, and the Chahtas slept upon their arms until morn. During the night, however, they held a council of war, and it was decided that the whole war party should go up the river, with the exception of a few spies, and conceal themselves in the thick cane above the falls, distant about two miles and a half. At the council it was asked in relation to the first charge that was made on the Muskogee lines in the canebrake during the battle of the day, who it was that led the little party? It was answered by those who were in a position to see the charge, that it was led by a strange, young looking man. And they said he went bounding into the charge more like the forcible leaping of a mad *koi* (panther) than a human being. The chief of the war party expressed a desire to see the young warrior if he could be found. The messenger who was sent to hunt the young man returned and reported that he has remained as a volunteer among the spies who had been detailed to watch the movements of the enemy.

They lay in the canebrake until daylight, when their spies came up and reported the Muskogees were crossing the river a mile below where they had the battle with them the day before and that they were in considerable force. The Chahtas formed the line of battle at a little creek a small distance below the falls and sending out a detachment of twenty men as an advance, waited till towards noon before they heard anything of what was going on. Then the advance picket came running back and reported the enemy close at hand. The chief ordered the advance to cross the branch and form behind the trees, and when the enemy came up to fire on them and run. And when the engagement took place for them to go up the little creek and charge them from behind if they could. Soon the advance of the enemy came up and a sharp skirmish took place between them and the Chahtas who had formed behind the trees, which continued until the main body came up. The Chahta skirmishers, in accordance with their instructions, on seeing the approach of the main body of the Muskogees, fled away, while their main force remained concealed in the gully of the little creek, not having fired a gun. As soon as the Chahta skirmishers fled, the Creeks (Muskogees) raised the war whoop, and penned them. When they came nearer the little creek the Chahtas opened a deadly fire on them, and they being so near there were but few shots lost. A great many of the Muskogees fell dead at the first fire, and while they were thus suddenly checked for a little time, the Chahtas had time to reload their guns and had commenced firing again. The Muskogees jumped behind the trees and the battle commenced in good earnest. The firing was not at this stage of the battle very constant. Each party were firing only when they could see a man, or a part of a man, to shoot at. Both parties held their position for a considerable length of time and notwithstanding that the Chahtas had at the first fire each killed or disabled his man or nearly so, the Muskogees still outnumbered them. This they could plainly understand from their yelling and the extent of ground they covered.

This state of affairs, however, was not destined to remain long. A shout was heard in the rear of the Muskogee forces, and soon there was a perceptible stir amongst them. They found themselves attacked with what from the yelling seemed to be a considerable force from behind, and they were about to make arrangements to meet it. But before they had affected anything a terrific shout was heard between them and the river. Neither party expected any aid from that direction and were alike at a loss to know who it should be. Soon the rush of yelling warriors explained the enigma to the astounded Muskogees. Wildly bounding into the very midst of their greatest force and strongest position came a band of ferocious warriors led by a man from whose eyes the fire seemed to flash, while with a ponderous war club, wielded by an arm potent in its irristible power, he hewed down man after man as he rushed from place to place. The men who came into the charge with him following his example were playing bloody havoc in all directions. At the same time the twenty warriors who had been ordered round from the front plunged into the fight from the rear. And now the main body of the Chahtas, who had all this time been concealed in the bed of the ravine, charged the enemy in front, and, with the shout of victory, fell in upon the confused and panic-stricken Muskogees who fell an easy prey to the victorious Chahtas. Very few made good their escape. With a few exceptions the whole party was slaughtered. They took no prisoners, and as the Muskogees were all armed with good rifles the plunder was valuable.

After they had driven the few that escaped from the slaughter across the river they returned to the battle-ground, secured the plunder, buried in secure places their own dead, and, not caring to cross the river to attack a town of women and children, they set out on the return march. The victory had been a signal and complete one, notwithstanding the loss of twenty-seven brave warriors whom they deeply mourned.

They camped the first night after the battle on Nuchuba, now called the Sipki River by the white people, about eight miles from the Tushkalusa River. After placing their pickets they assembled around a council fire and recounted the results of the two battles. A great many war achievements were described and war names conferred, but all agreed that the daring and irresistible charges of a certain young warrior, whom no one could tell the name of, or where he came from, had eclipsed them all.

The chief sent for the mysterious young warrior, and when he came to the council fire he was but a calm, sedate and quite pleasant looking young man, having nothing in his appearance that would seem to vindicate the fearless action and rushing intrepidity that he had so daringly manifested in the hour of battle. No person present knew him. The chief asked of him from what town he came. He replied calmly that he did not reside in a town. Then, from what land did you come? He answered quickly, "From the Chahta country." The chief, somewhat perplexed, inquired of him if he would have any objections to giving his name. He answered:

"None at all. Until a few winters ago, while participating, for the first time in my life, in a hunting party in the Mississippi bottoms, I was at first called the 'nameless strippling,' and some of the party, in derision I suppose, regaled themselves by calling me 'Bony.' Afterwards, while we were still prosecuting the hunt, for reasons best known to themselves, the party, seemingly by unanimous consent, took it into their heads to bestow on me the highly reputable name of 'Ishtilauata,' and by that name, with that party, I have been known ever since. With other parties and people I had no name."

"Have you not kindred, relations?" inquired the chief.

"None that I know of," said the young warrior.

"Then," returned the chief, "I am to understand from your answers to my questions that you do belong to a Chahta country, but that you have no particular home place, no relatives, nor any name except that which the hunters gave you in the only hunting expedition in which you have participated."

"That," rejoined the young warrior, "is the meaning of my answers to your interrogatories, and it is the truth, with the exception that you have made a mistake that the hunting party alluded to was my only participation with a party of hunters, when I intended you to understand that it was my first expedition with a company of bear hunters. Previous to that time, notwithstanding the fact that from my earliest recollections I had extracted from the forests and water courses my entire subsistence by my skill with the blow gun and bow, I had never taken part in a camp hunt with a company of hunters before. I dwelled alone in the wild forests and dark swamp lands, with only an occasional transient associate, until I thought I had grown to be a man, when I joined the before named company of hunters on the evening of their first day's travel towards the Mississippi bottom, where they spent the winter in a successful bear hunt, as I thought, and there was where I accumulated the distinguished appellation of 'Brag,' as I before stated."

"The history you give of yourself," said the chief, "is strange. You give no account of your origin; no mention is made of your mother or even the iksa from which you sprang; you do not even seem to know that you had a name previous to your expedition with the hunters in the Mississippi bottoms. It is, to say the least of it, an extraordinary story and your prowess in battle is equally extraordinary. Clear up the enigma which is presented in the history you give of yourself and the daring exploits you so well managed at the proper time in our late battle and it will entitle you to a big war name."

"I have told you all I know about myself," said the young man, while the fire began to flash from his steady eyes, "and as for what you are pleased to refer to as daring exploits in battle, they were not performed in anticipation of an honorable war name, but to subdue the enemies of my country. But I find from what you have said to me to-night that it is not the actual demonstration of timely and sufficient aid in the time of peril that will entitle a man to honor in your estimation, but to the history of his origin, parentage, iksa, etc. From my very soul I detest all such titles, and I beseech you to forbear the bestowal of a war name upon me at this time or any other time upon such terms."

And turning away quickly he left the council and was not seen again during that expedition. Nor did he appear at the great war dance which took place on the return of the war party.

The war continuing with the Muskogees it was not long till the intrepid young warrior was leading a party of terrible warriors of his own selection, and they were making repeated successful forages upon the borders of the Creek country. Very soon his fame as a great leader and invincible warrior was spread over the whole Chahta country, and to the Muskogee people the reputation of his name filled every breast with terror.

He had at last consented, at the solicitation at one of their great *Ishtahullo,* to receive a war name. It was the custom in those days for the *Ishtahullo,* high priest or chaplain, who always accompanied and conjured for the war parties, to confer the way name. There was much mystery in the manner the *Ishtahullo* conjured out a war name. He carried a leather bag in which was deposited thirteen smooth stones, or pebbles, of various colors. And when any one performed a feat in battle that merited a war name, the *Ishtahullo* would, by his conjuration, select from the bag one of his mysterious pebbles, and from the impression he received on hearing the history of the war story and in conjuring out the stone, he would utter the war name. Our hero, Ishtilauata, had performed many daring feats in battle, and had drawn stone after stone from the *Ishtahullo* until he had got them all. But he would not then consent to receive a war name. He raised another party and made a furious forage upon the Muskogee towns, where he distinguished himself more by his won-derful daring and success in taking scalps than he had ever before done. When the battle was over he went to the *Ishtahullo* and very calmly remarked:

"I am ready to receive a war name now."
The priest replied, "There is no more in the bag. You have, by your numerous brave exploits in battle taken them all out."
After conjuring a while, however, the priest came back and said: "I shall confer upon you, and it is because you have clearly and fairly won it, the most distinguished and the greatest war name that has

ever been conferred upon any warrior of any nation. Your war name shall be, and it is a very significant appellation, Apushimataha" (no more in the bag). The warrior then bowed his head and repeated "Apushimataha! Fihopa" (I am content).

Apushimataha, the name by which he was ever afterwards known, soon became a very conspicuous character, and was the main leader of the war parties in the war against the Muskogee nations. His efforts in this expeditions against the Creeks were universally crowned with success. And such was the terror of his name that the Muskogees had ceased to make incursions west of the boundary lines between the two nations or to hunt on the disputed territory which lay in the fork of the Tushkalusa and Tombigbee rivers.

They were considered a conquered people, and Apushimataha, still active and ambitious, conceived the idea of seeking fame with a braver and more noble foe. He set himself to work and soon succeeded in raising a very large war party, with the intention of making war upon the Ovashsashi nation. He had not forgotten the manner in which they had treated his war companions that he had accompanied in his youthful days to that country, and he made that an excuse for making war upon them. In his speeches while beating up for volunteers he never failed to narrate the affair of the lime sink and the smoky cave. Now two hundred and eighty-four Ovashsashis yelled and raved around the little lime sink that contained only thirty-nine half famished Chahtas, half a night and half a day, lost four of their own warriors and effected nothing more than to give the Chahtas a pretty smart smoking.

In the form he put it up it was a popular story, and he succeeded in organizing quite an army of warriors to go against the warlike Ovashsashis.

The party was well equipped, having good rifles, plenty of powder and lead, and each man carried, by order of Apushimataha, nearly half a bushel of *Tan'bota* (cold flour). The cold flour was to be held in reserve and only to be resorted to when they could find no game on the route. The plan was to take time and supply themselves by hunting as they traveled. All being ready, they set out, three hundred and twenty strong, at the time the strawberries and early spring fruits had begun to ripen. And crossing the Mississippi above the mouth of the Arkansa River, they made their way in three parties in the direction of the Ovashsashi country. Each division had a leader assigned it, who was acquainted with the country, and he was instructed to steer his course to a certain point far up the Neosho River, where the division that arrives first was to remain until the remainder should come up. Each division was conducted by good leaders, and the whole party met again in thirty-four days.

They were now not far from the Ovashsashi country, and sending out a few spies to ascertain the locality of their hunting parties, the Chahtas remained on the Neosho River, killing and drying the buffalo meat until the spies should return. They found the buffaloes plenty, and they prepared, by drying, as much meat as they could pack.

At the end of ten sleeps the spies returned and reported that they had discovered two parties of hunters, one of them very large, the other did not consist of exceeding a hundred men. Both camps were of the Ovashsashi people and had their families with them.

Apushimataha decided to attack the larger camp and immediately made arrangements for that purpose. Having the direction pointed out to him his plan was soon arranged and made known to his leaders and captains, who received the orders with manifestations of great satisfaction. The force was divided into three columns, with an experienced warrior chief to each division. The divisions were subdivided into bands of twenties with a leader to each band. The programme laid down by Apushimataha for the movement of the three divisions was the following: The first division was to go to the left and to diverge wide enough from the direct course to the Ovashsashi camp to avoid being discovered by their hunting parties; the third division was ordered to the right and to follow the same instruction. The second division, commanded by Apushimataha in person, was to remain one day in camp after the other two divisions had marched, and then go forward on a straight line to the Ovashsashi camps. The first division was to pass on, if they could do so without being discovered, until their spies had informed them that they were far enough to attack the camp in a quartering direction from beyond. The third division received instructions to make the attack in the same way from the right. He then told them that the second division would be at the right place at the right time. The first and third divisions, as soon as it was dark, moved forward. The second division waited to move forward the next night, which they did.

The Ovashsashi camp lay from the Chahta camp on the Neosho about three days' traveling to the northwest and contained from the best estimate the spies could make, five or six hundred warriors. The Chahta columns were ordered to travel only at night, and to move forward with the greatest caution. It would require four nights and a half for the flanking columns to make the trip and for the center division, if they were not discovered, three nights. Orders were for them to make the attack at daybreak on the fifth morning. All understood the entire plan and the right and left columns moved forward in accordance with their instructions.

They diverged widely, and making forced marches found themselves at the designated points by the middle of the fourth night. Their sagacious spies told them they could rest a little while and then make the trip to the Ovashsashi camp by daybreak. By the spies the first and third divisions had already communicated and were moving in concert.

The Ovashsashi camp lay upon the valley of a considerable creek, and was stretched along its banks for more than a mile. There was now a great deal of timber, cotton wood, elm, etc. all growing very near the banks of the creek. All this had been described by the spies and was perfectly understood by the Chahtas. And as they drew near each division threw out, every little while, bands of twenty toward the center of the encampment, with orders to take distance rapidly until the first twenty came in sight of the deploying bands of the other divisions. And when they reached the brow of the declivity which overhangs the valley of the encampment to sit down and wait for the signal. The whole movement was admirably performed and the entire number of the warriors of the two divisions were seated before the day had peeped, in sullen silence, on the brow of the hill which overlooked the encampment of the unsuspecting Ovashsashis. On the brink of that little hill, crouched in the obscurity of the night, was the long line of dark spirits, each one firmly grasping his deathly weapon, while his savage heart throbbed with delight in anticipation of the scenes of blood so near at hand.

At the first gleam of the morning light the signal owl hooting passed along the line, and instantly the charge, accompanied by the terrific war whoop, resounded along the whole line of the rushing warriors. Onward they wildly dashed, right towards the camp fires. It was but a short run.

It had so happened that morning that a large party of the Ovashsashi warriors, for the purpose of surprising a herd of buffalo not far off, had risen very early and were at the time of the charge all armed and ready to start in the hunt. They quickly strung their bows and welcomed the Chahtas with a shower of arrows, killing several and wounding a good many more. The Chahtas immediately commenced firing upon them, and, being so near, almost every shot took deadly effect. The Ovashsashis greatly outnumbering them, plied their arrows incessantly, and were performing a deadly work, thinning the Chahta ranks rapidly. The chiefs, seeing that they were about to be overpowered by superior numbers, ordered a charge, and soon both parties were mixed up in a hand to hand conflict. The Chahtas all had fine large knives, while the Ovashsashis had nothing to fight with in close combat except the sticks from their meat scaffolds and a few hatchets. These they gathered and were contending bravely against the sharp knives of the Chahtas. The battle was raging madly and the Chahtas, though they were killing some one every time, and had the advantage in weapons, yet under the pressure of the vastly superior numbers of the foe, they were beginning to waver. Some of them had withdrawn a little distance and had commenced firing again. And notwithstanding that every fire told on the enemy, it was too slow and did not seem to do much good in a battle of this kind. There was no chance for escape and nobody thought of trying it. All were determined to sell their lives as dearly as possible and now when every nerve and thought was strained to its utmost tension, when the result of the battle seemed to be oscillating, and all was dire war struggle, a sound of a sweeping tornado seemed to quiver through the din and uproar of the bloody conflict. Soon the sound came again, more startling than before. The Ovashsashi warriors suspended operations a moment to listen. Wildly and more terrific than ever the sound came again. Terror stricken they cast their eyes around for a moment as if uncertain what course to pursue. But before they had time to come to any conclusion the storm of war was assailing them from the opposite side of their camp. The loud shout of recognition greeted the wavering spirits of the tired warriors of the first and third divisions. And now, sweeping down the hill from the opposite side of the creek, like the rushing waters of the irresistible mountain torrent, came the second division, led by the furious Apushimataha. They rushed very near to the creek and opened a terrible fire on the Ovashsashis. The first and third divisions then drew back a little and opened fire also. The Chahtas all had white feathers in their hair, and now the sun being an hour high, it was an easy matter to distinguish them from the Ovashsashi warriors, who were now in utter dismay between the deadly fire of the Chahta forces. Having previously shot all their arrows away they were reduced to a defenseless condition. Panic stricken they began to jump into the bed of the creek and were trying to escape by running along in the water. But the Chahtas, seeing this, charged up to the banks of the creek and shooting them from both sides filled the water with dead men for more than a mile. None who ran into the creek made good their escape. If any of that great number of mighty warriors got away, they must have effected it in the early stages of the sanguinary battle. Some of the women and children had been accidentally killed in the furious battle, but most of them had escaped by running off down the opposite bank of the creek at the first onset before it was light enough to see them.

The Chahtas took no prisoners, and when the work of death was completed, they all went up the creek above the encampment in search of clear water, for they were all very thirsty. After resting awhile they took some refreshments, and then proceeded to scalp and enumerate the dead. They found 509 dead Ovashsashis, sixty-three dead Chahtas and eighty-seven wounded, some of them badly.

They buried their dead the same day, and before the next morning three of their wounded had died, and as soon as they had interred them, the balance of the wounded being able to walk, they set out towards the other encampment that had been reported by the spies. They traveled till evening, when they struck up camp and after refreshing themselves a little, leaving the wounded with a small guard, the efficient warriors, 150 in number, set out, making forced marches by night, until they came in striking distance of the camp. They made reconnoisances by scouting parties, who soon returned and reported the condition of the camp. They gave a description of its surroundings, and the number of warriors, which they supposed to be about 130.

Apushimataha immediately divided his men into bands of tens, and, putting a brave leader over each band, ordered them to deploy to the right and left, with instructions to surround the camp and to be ready for the attack by daybreak, when he would himself give the signal for the onset. His programme was successfully carried out, and the whole of his forces were drawn up in sight of the camp fires and resting upon their arms before the day dawned. Just as the morning birds began to chirp a party of Ovashsashi hunters, who were hurrying out on an early hunt, came in contact with one of the Chahta bands. The Chahtas hailed them, and as they did not speak, the Chahtas fired upon them, killing most of them upon the spot. Those who had escaped ran back to the camp to find their comrades in great trepidation and confusion. All was bustle and hurry; few could find their arms to meet the onslaught that was rushing upon them from every direction. The terrible war whoop and the sharp, mad cracks of the rifles of the invaders filled every heart with dismay, and they seemed to hurdle in bunches about their camp. The light of the morning was every moment becoming brighter, and the effect of the pealing rifles was constantly increasing and more deadly. Now was seen running through their panic stricken ranks their tall, fine-formed chief; he was a brave man, and with all the powers of his dauntless spirit was endeavoring to restore order and courage to his greatly confused and hopeless warriors. His presence produced an instant movement among them. Now that they could see more distinctly their courage began to return to them, and gathering up their weapons raised the loud defiant war shout, and their sharp, flint pointed arrows were soon filling the air with their deathly whizzing sounds. For a little time the contest seemed to balance. Apushimataha having discovered the nodding feather that decorated the brow of the tall, well-formed chief, fiercely bounded into his presence and, stopping for an instant, seemed to greet the magnificent warrior with a smile of admiration. The tall Ovashsashi chief drew down his brow and, looking upon the much less form of Apushimataha with scowling contempt, swung high in the air his ponderous war club, making a sweeping pass with it at the head of Apushimataha, who received it glancing up the barrel of his rifle, which he held in his left hand, and at the same moment, quick as the lightning's flash, stove his long knife through the temple bone and deep into the brain of the mighty warrior chief. His large, muscular form paralyzed, plunged to the ground, when his invincible conqueror, with the fire of triumph flashing from his eyes, leaped upon the prostrate giant, and deliberately removed that portion of his scalp which contained the feathers. Then, standing erect on the still quivering frame of the fallen chief, and waving high above his head, on the point of his knife, the feather-adorned scalp, he shouted aloud, with his peculiar harsh, jarring, terrific voice, a sound that no one could or ever attempted to imitate, calling on his brave followers to rush to the slaughter, "the victory is ours." Then instantly whirling from his elevated position, with the bounding strength and activity of the mad panther, he plunged wildly into the thickest of the fray. Encouraged by his extraordinary daring and inimitable prowess, his warriors dashed into the camp from every quarter. The Ovashsashi warriors had witnessed the fall of their beloved chief, and that unfortunate disaster and the sudden rush upon them from every direction by the furious warriors of the exultant foe, filled them with dire consternation, and although a portion of them continued to battle bravely, they soon fell an easy prey to the superior weapons of the triumphant Chahtas. The battle was finished by an indiscriminate slaughter. Neither man, woman nor child was left alive to tell the news of that dreadful day.

The Chahta warriors scalped all the slain, numbering 381. Their own loss amounted to thirteen killed and twenty-nine wounded, only one dangerously.

Both the camps they had taken were full of rich plunder, but being so far from home and having so many wounded men, they did not appropriate any of it except a few dressed deer skins and some curiosities peculiar to the Ovashsashi people. They went far enough up the little creek upon which the slaughtered camp lay to be out of reach of the offensive stench and to attend to their wounded, and, resting two or three days, encamped in a pleasant little elm grove near to the water. They also sent a runner to bring forward the wounded who had been left behind. Other parties went down and brought up to the new camps great quantities of nicely cured buffalo meat and some kind of meat that was beaten to powder and put up in leather bags. It was very good, but they did not know to what animal it belonged. It was conveniently fixed for traveling provision and for that purpose they preserved it.

In four days the wounded had recovered so far as to be able to travel. The well men were so heavily packed carrying provisions for the wounded that they were compelled to leave all the guns of their dead warriors and some of those belonging to the wounded, who were too feeble to carry anything. They threw the surplus guns into a deep hole in the creek to prevent the Ovashsashis from finding them, and, all being satisfied with the success of the expedition, they turned their faces homeward. As the weather was now very warm and some of their wounded quite weak and feverish they chose the night to travel in; and so at the twilight of the fifth night they left the new camp and, moving off slowly, heavily tramped the grassy plain until near daybreak, when, coming to a small rivulet of good water shaded by a heavy grove of trees they concluded to lay down their packs and rest until the cool of the ensuing evening. And thus they continued to lie in camp during the day and travel of nights until they had passed the confines of the Ovashsashi country, when they, after selecting a convenient camping place, rested until all the wounded had recovered.

During this detention their hunters had laid in a full supply of fresh meat, which was nicely dried at the camp fires, and packed up for the journey. They set out one fair morning and continued to travel day after day until they reached their respective homes. News of the great victory was sent out to all the neighboring towns and a day was appointed to celebrate a great war dance. The dance took place on Buckatunna, a small river not far from the town in which the most of the warriors that had participated in the late expedition resided. There was a great turn-out and the dance continued three days. They had suspended their 890 scalps on poles in the dance ground. The people counted them and were greatly astonished. They said the like had never been known before, and that the great chief, Apushimataha, as no one could tell from whence he came, must have been sent by the *shilombish chito,* and to destroy the enemies of the Chahta people.

On the first day of the dance Apushimataha made his appearance for the first time at a war dance. But when the orators began to make speeches and to eulogize the great invincible war chief he stealthily glided away and was no more seen at that celebration.

The fame of Apushimataha had reached every portion of the Chahta nation long previous to this wonderful expedition against the Ovashsashi people. And now after his return from that far-off country, bringing back with him nearly a thousand scalps of that exceedingly large and war-like nation, nobody else was talked of. He had become the theme in all their orations and the nations' heart had turned towards and was set upon him as the man who had been sent among them to conquer and drive all enemies of the Chahtas far away from their boundaries.

Apushimataha was not only the idol of his own people, but he had many distinguished friends among his white acquaintances at Mobile among the Spaniards and trading adventurers of other nations, and among the United States officers at Fort Confederation on the Tombeckbee River. The old chief of the district to which he belonged, Tuscona Hopaia, had called upon him and offered to resign his chiefship to him. But to this Apushimataha would by no means consent. He was, however, dubbed chief everywhere he went by all the districts and was looked upon as chief by everybody. When Brigadier General James Wilkinson, commissioner for holding con-

ferences with the Indian nation south of the Ohio River called on
him as chief at a treaty held at Fort Confederation on the subject
of retracing the boundaries, in 1802, to sign the articles, he denied
being chief and would not make his mark until Tuscona Hopaia,
who was the chief of that district, and two distinguished leaders,
had made their marks. There being four names required he would
not sign till the last. When the old chief, Tuscona Hopaia, died, by
general consent the district made him chief by acclamation, without
consulting him on the subject at all. He yielded to their wishes; they
continued to elect him every four years and he faithfully served them
as long as he lived.

Soon after he was made chief he attended a treaty of limits between the United States and the Chahta nation, held in Pushapuknuk in the Chahta country, by James Robertson and Silas Dinsmore, commissioners on the part of the United States, and the three
chiefs of the nations, Apukshinubi and Mingo Homastubi and our
hero, Apushimataha. This treaty took place in the autumn of 1805.
Apushimataha took a very active part in this treaty, making many
speeches, contesting with great force several propositions made by
the United States' commissioners. And in all part of the stipulations
he manifested the signs of deep thought and of perfect knowledge
of the topics that were discussed. He obtained for the scraps of land
cut off from the Chahta country by this treaty $50,500 to pay the
debts of the Chahta people, due from them to the merchants and
traders with whom they had been dealing; and $2,500 to John
Pitchlynn, United States interpreter, for his services rendered to
the United States and for losses he had sustained, besides an annual stipend for the use of the nation of $3,000 to be paid in such
goods as the chiefs should designate, at Philadelphia prices. To this
annuity they did not prescribe a limit. He also at this treaty obtained for each chief $500 paid down in specie and an annuity of
$150 each during their continuance in office. The commissioners also
bestowed on him a heavy medal, which he received without com-
ment, and signed the treaty, last among the chiefs, remarking that
the other two had been in office longer than he had. In 1816 at a
treaty held at the Chahta trading house by John Coffee, John Rhea

and John McKee, commissioners on the part of the United States, the three medal chiefs and a number of leaders and warriors on the part of the Chahtas for the cession of half that tract of country lying in the fork of the Tombeckbee and Tuscaloosa rivers, that had been the cause of so many years' war between the Muskogees and the Chahta nations, Apushimataha was as usual the speaking advocate for the rights of the Chahta people, and he managed by his eloquent speeches and diplomatic tact to obtain a pretty fair remuneration for the disputed territory. He obtained from the United States an annual payment of $6,000 in cash and $10,000 in merchandise, which was to be paid immediately on signing the treaty. The treaty was signed and sealed and the goods delivered as fast as possible from the stock of goods then at the trading house.

At a treaty held by General Jackson and General Hinds at Doak Stand, in the Chahta country, during the autumn of 1820, Apushimataha distinguished himself greatly with the two generals by his extraordinary powers; his very correct knowledge of the geography of the far-off country west of the Mississippi River and his astonishing eloquence. They had three excellent interpreters, John Pitchlynn, Middleton Mackey and Edmund Fulsome. All he said was clearly and fairly rendered in good English and General Jackson declared that his speeches on that occasion would have done honor to any man of the age. He regretted that he had not prepared himself with a reporter, as his inimitable figures so beautifully niched in the immense fabric of his exceedingly fine Chahta oratory were certainly a regretable loss to the literary world. The object the United States had in holding this treaty was to exchange, if they could, all that country where the Chahta and Chickasaw nations now reside and claim west of the Mississippi River for a slip of territory from the lower part of the then Chahta nation, known as the Big Black country, in the State of Mississippi.

General Jackson had conferred the appointment of Brigadier General on Apushimataha, who, with a brigade of Chahta warriors, had served under Jackson during the war of 1818 against the Creeks, Mikisukies and Alocheway Indians. He was at the taking of Fort Baranchas, Pensacola and Mobile, distinguishing himself as a discreet commander and courageous warrior. General Jackson was familiarly acquainted with him, and in his opening speech at the treaty ground seemed to point his discourse mainly to Apushimataha, addressing him in the friendly epithet of "Brother Push." A large portion of the nation was in attendance, and after General Jackson had read the commission and the President's letter to them, in a long speech he opened up the object and purposes for which the people of the great and ever friendly nation of Chahtas had been called together. He declared to that very large assembly in which could be seen the faces of many white people who had attended the treaty, "that to promote the civilization of the Chahta people by the establishment of schools among them and to perpetuate them as a nation was a subject of constant solicitude with the President of the United States. It was an object near to his heart.

To enable the President to effectuate this great national and very desirable object, to accommodate the growing State of Mississippi, and thereby secure greater safety and protection to the Chahtas and their seminaries of learning at home, it was proposed by him to exchange for a small part of their land here a large country beyond the Mississippi River where all, who live by hunting and will not work, and who by the nature of their mode of life are widely scattered, may be collected and settled together in a country of tall trees, many water courses, rich lands and high grass abounding in game of all kinds—buffalo, bear, elk, deer, antelope, beaver, turkeys, honey and fruits of many kinds. In this great hunting ground they might be settled near together for protection and be able to pursue their peculiar vocation without danger.

Another great benefit to be derived from this arrangement would be the removal from among the people at home who are already inclined to progress and civilization of the bad example of those who, in their wild, wandering propensities, do not care for improvement. The project recommended itself to the thinking portion of the industrious community while it would provide ample means for the protection of the careless stragglers of the nation.

The tract of territory which the President proposed to exchange for the Big Black country lay between the Arkansas and Red rivers; it is a large and extensive country. Beginning where the lower boundary line of the Cherokees strikes the Arkansas River, thence up the Canadian to its source, thence due south to the Red River, thence down the Red River to a point three miles below the mouth of Little River, which empties into Red River from the north, thence on a direct line to the beginning.

This extensive rich territory, they were told, was offered in exchange by the President for the little slip of land at the lower part of the present Chahta nation. It is a much larger territory than the whole of the Chahta possessions this side of the Mississippi River' and was certainly a very liberal proposition. They were asked, "What say the chiefs and Chahta people to this great offer?" '

After the pipe lighters had finished handing the pipes around and order was restored, Apushimataha arose, and addressing himself to his own people first, told them that the man who had just finished his big talk was the great warrior, General Jackson, whom they all had so often heard of, many of them had no doubt seen him and like himself had served under him in many successful battles. His great character as a man and a warrior, in addition to the commission he bore from the President of the United States, demanded from the Chahta people respectful replies to his propositions, and for that purpose he moved that the council adjourn until the middle of the day to-morrow, which motion was carried and the council adjourned accordingly.

The chiefs and headmen went into a secret council that night where they very deliberately discussed the merits of the proposition that had been made by the United States commissioners. They considered it a wise and benevolent proposition, and notwithstanding the land they offered to exchange the large tract of western territory for was worth more to them at this time than two such countries as the one they were offering, with the Chahtas the thing stood very different, particularly in relation to the fixing of a home for the wandering hunters in the midst of a game country. However good as the proposition was they decided that they must in this case adopt the white man's rules in the transaction and get all they could from them. They recognized the fact that General Jackson was a great

man, but in his talk in making the proposition to exchange countries they said he had been guilty of misrepresentations which he
knew were such, and others which he was not perhaps apprised of.
Their plan was to meet him in the treaty with his own policy and
let the hardest reap the profits. If they could do no better they
would accept the offer already made. This much and the appointment of Apushimataha to do the talking next day was the result of
the secret council.

When at twelve o'clock the next day the council assembled the
commissioners enquired of the chiefs if they had come to any conclusions on the subject of the proposition made to them yesterday
in relation to the exchange of countries. Apushimataha arose and
said that the chiefs and leaders of his country had appointed him to
reply to the commissioners on that subject. He remarked that he
fully appreciated the magnitude of the proposition and his incom-
petency to do it justice, especially while in contact with two such
master minds as he would have to deal with. He further remarked
that when any business was intended to be fairly and honestly trans-
acted it made no difference as to the capacity of the contracting
parties. One party might be as great a man as General Jackson, the
other a fool, but the result would be the same. The wise man, in
such cases would protect the rights of the fool, holding him firm
on the safe ground. From what he had already heard he had discovered that this great transaction, now about to take place between
friendly nations, who dwell almost in mixed society together, was
not to be conducted on those equitable principles and that it would
not be safe for him, fool as he was, to rely upon such expectation.
He was to come to the contest with such powers as he possesses, do
the best he could, and his people must be satisfied and abide the
results. The object and benefits to be derived by the United States
were great and very desirable or they would not have sent two of
their greatest warrior generals to conduct the treaty in their behalf.
He was friendly towards the United States, and particularly so to
their two distinguished agents, for he had served under and side by
side with them in the hour of peril and deathly strife, and had aided
them in the acquisition of Florida and a considerable portion of

the Muskogee country with his manhood, as had as many of his
countrymen as he could persuade to take part in the dangers of
the enterprise. Under all these considerations he intended to strike
the bargain in the exchange of countries with them if he could.
He thought it was one of those kind of swaps if it could be fairly
made that it would accommodate both parties. He should do his
best and he hoped to succeed in presenting the thing in such form
as to convince the commissioners that further misrepresentation
would be entirely unnecessary. He then took his seat calmly, without
even a glance from his eyes either towards the red or the white audi-
ences, when General Jackson rose and gravely remarked: "Brother
Push, you have uttered some hard words. You have openly accused
me of misrepresentation and indirectly of the desire to defraud the
red people in behalf of my government. These are heavy charges,
charges of a very serious character. You must explain yourself in a
manner that will clear them up or I shall quit you."

Apushimataha arose, took the speakers' stand very deliberately
and casting his eyes, which were now beaming with the light that
fired his great soul, upon his audience, said:

> "As men grow older, especially great men, enthralling themselves
> with much business on the field of growing fame, they become im-
> patient and irritable. They dare not stop on the path of their rushing
> and varying necessities to parley with the ignorant. They must make
> short work with all such obstructions. There is no honor in permit-
> ting the feeble or the foolish he may meet in his precipitate course
> to pass. No allowance is to be made or forgiveness offered for him.
> He must yield to the mere say so of the warily moving seeker of
> fame or be crushed. I have been making observation on that cast of
> character a long time, and find but little difference in their public
> action. In their private intercourse the whole thing is changed.
>
> "My great friend, General Jackson, who familiarly calls me brother,
> whom my inner soul loveth, and in whose presence I always felt my-
> self a mere boy, has become excited at some of my remarks, and has
> hastily called on me to explain them, and that explanation must be
> satisfactory of he will 'quit us,' the meaning of which, as I suppose,
> is that should I fail to make the *amende honorable* he returns to his
> government and informs them that the insulting obstinacy of the
> Chahta people is such that an honorable treaty cannot be negotiated

with them. Then comes the horrors of war against us. All I have to say about it is that I hope they will have the good sense and the justice to put it upon those only who have raised the fuss to do the fighting. It would indeed be a great error in the justice of any government to involve the innocent inhabitants of two nations in the ruinous consequences of war on account of a misunderstanding betwixt two of their ministers.

"You gentlemen, General Jackson and General Hinds, are filling, as I understand from the letter you read before the council yesterday, the place of commissioners from the government of the United States to hold a treaty for certain purposes with the people of the Chahta country. Am I right?" and both the generals nodding assent, Apushimataha resumed and said: "I informed you in the outset, which I here repeat, that I occupy the same position. I, too, have been appointed by my government as commissioner to hold a treaty through you gentlemen with your people. I am therefore your equal, as far as appointment can make us so. I have already recognized your appointment and authority as being in all respects on an equal basis with my own. You, gentlemen, must reciprocate." And he seated himself on the bench with the commissioners, looking remarkably sedate.

General Jackson, in a remarkably good humor, rose and said: "General Apushimataha, in all respects in this treaty we acknowledge you to be vested with powers equal to ourselves and precisely on the same footing in relation to your country that we are to ours. You shall have no complaint to make against us in that respect. And now, as we are all equals, not of our own creation, but by the appointment of our respective nations, you are in a condition to go on and explain wherein I have misrepresented any fact in the propositions I have made in the name of my government. The nature of our position demands it, and we expect it from you."

Apushimataha said: "I shall take much pleasure in my explanation to render a plain and irrefutable interpretation of what I have said, and I will present in a very clear light the misrepresentations in relation to the quality of the country west of the Mississippi and the size of the country outside of the great river by my highly esteemed friend.

"In the first place he speaks of the country he wishes to obtain in the swap as 'a little slip of land at the lower part of the present Chahta nation,' whereas it is a very considerable tract of country. He has designated the boundaries of it himself, and I am very familiar with the entire tract of land it will cut off from us. In the sec-

ond place, he represented the country he wishes to exchange for the
'little slip' as being a very extensive country 'of tall trees, many water
courses, rich lands and high grass, abounding in game of all kinds—
buffalo, bear, elk, deer, antelope, beaver, turkeys, honey and fruits
of many kinds.' I am also well acquainted with that country. I have
hunted there often, have chased the Comanchee and the Ovashsashi
over those endless plains, and they have sometimes chased me there.
I know the country well. It is indeed a very extensive land, but a vast
amount of it is exceedingly poor and sterile, trackless, sandy deserts,
nude of vegetation of any kind. As to tall trees, there is no timber
anywhere except on the bottom lands, and it is low and boukey even
there. The grass is everywhere very short, and for the game it is not
plenty, except buffalo and deer. The buffalo in the western portion
of the tract described and on the great plains into which it reaches
are very numerous and easily taken; antelope, too, are there and deer
almost everywhere except in the dry, grassless, sandy deserts. There
are but few elk, and the bear are plenty only on Red River bottom
lands. Turkeys are plentiful on all the water courses. There are, however, but few beavers, and the honey and fruit are rare things. The
bottoms on the rivers are generally good soil, but liable to inundation
during the spring season, and in summers the rivers and creeks dry
up or become so salt that the water is awful for use. It is not at these
times always salt, but often bitter, and will purge a man like medicine. This account differs widely from the description given by my
friend yesterday and constitutes what in my reply to him I styled a
misrepresentation. He has proven to me by that misrepresentation
and one egregious error that he is entirely ignorant of the geography
of the country he is offering to swap, and therefore I shall acquit
him of an intention at fraud. The testimony that he bears against
himself in regard to his deficiency of a knowledge of the geography
of that far off country manifests itself in the fact that he has offered
to swap to me an undefined portion of Mexican territory. He offers
to run the line up the Canadian River to its source and thence due
south to Red River. Now I know that a line running due south from
the source of the Canadian would never touch any portion of Red
River, but would go into the Mexican possessions beyond the limits
even of my geographical knowledge."

General Jackson, interrupting him, said: "See here, Brother Push,
you must be mistaken. Look at this map; it will prove to you at once
that you are laboring under a great geographical error yourself;" and
he spread out the map.

Apushimataha examined it very minutely while General Jackson traced out and read the names of the rivers for him. Apushimataha said, "the paper is not true." He then proceeded to mark out on the ground with the handle of the pipe hatchet which he held in his hand while speaking, the Canadian and the upper branches of Red River and said, holding the end of the hatchet handle on the ground:

"Here is the south, and you see the line between the two points do not touch any portion of Red River, and I declare to you that that is the natural position of the country and its water course."

"You must be mistaken," said General Jackson; "at any rate I am willing to make good the proposition I have named."

"Very well," replied Apushimataha, "and you must not be surprised nor think hard of me if I point your attention to another subject within the limits of the country you have designated west of the Mississippi which you do not seem to be apprised of. The lower portion of the land you propose to swap is a pretty good country. It is true that as high up the Arkansas River as Forth Smith the lands are good and timber and water plenty; but there is an objectionable difficulty lying in the way. It was never known before in any treaty made by the United States with the red people that their commissioners were permitted to offer to swap off or sell any portion of their citizens. What I ask to know in the stipulations of the present treaty is whether the American settlers you propose to turn over to us in this exchange of countries are, when we get them in possession, to be considered Indians or white people?"

General Jackson rejoined and told the speaking chief that "As for the white people on the land it was a mere matter of moonshine. There were perhaps a few hunters scattered over the country, and he would have them ordered off."

"I beg your pardon," replied Apushimataha. "There are a great many of them, many of them substantial, well to do settlers, with good houses and productive farms, and they will not be ordered off."

"But," replied General Jackson, "I will send my warriors, and by the eternal I'll drive them into the Mississippi or make them leave it."

"Very well," replied the chief; and now the matter is settled as far as the land west of the great river is concerned. We will next consider the boundary and country the Chahtas are to give you for it, and if we can agree upon that the trade will be completed. You have defined its boundaries, and they include a very valuable tract of country, of considerable extent, capable of producing corn, cotton, wheat and all the crops the white man cultivates. Now, if we do agree on terms and run this line, it must, as a part of this contract, be very clearly understood, and put on paper in a form that will not die nor wear out, that no other alteration shall be made in the boundaries of that portion of our territory that will remain until the Chahta people are sufficiently progressed in the arts of civilization to become citizens of the State, owning land and homes of their own, on an equal footing with the white people. Then it may be surveyed and the surplus sold for the benefit of the Chahta people."

"That," said General Jackson, "is a magnificent arrangement, and we consent to it readily."

The day being well spent he proposed to the chiefs an adjournment until eleven o'clock the next day. It would give the chiefs and warriors time to discuss and arrange the details of the treaty and opportunity to his secretary for preparing his big paper upon which the articles and stipulations of the great contract between two friendly nations should be placed.

The chiefs assenting, an adjournment took place immediately.

The chiefs and people were highly pleased with the proceedings of the day and they went into secret council where they agreed and arranged what they intended to demand in detail to finish the swap, and put it on Apushimataha to do the talking again the coming day. They were all of opinion that the treaty would be finished in one more day and that it would result favorably to the red people they did not seem to doubt.

As soon as the council opened the next day General Hinds addressed a very friendly talk to the assembled nation. He spoke in the highest terms of their orderly behavior and their friendly deportment. He remarked that it was not only so with their own people, but the smiles and uninterrupted good humor with everybody on the ground was a subject worthy of praise. He said he had been in attendance at many gatherings of the white people, even in their legislative bodies and the great Congress of the United States, and he frankly confessed that he had never witnessed a single instance

that would compare with this. It was the first Indian council he had
ever had the good fortune to witness. And so long as he lived he
expected to refer to it as a model assembly of order, decency, friendship, sobriety and all that is necessary to assemblies. He declared
that he had never seen a larger assembly so well conducted in any
country or people, and closed his speech by enquiring of the chiefs
if they had any further propositions to make in relation to the
treaty.

Apushimataha replied: "I have a few more points to introduce for
the consideration of the commissioners, and I make no doubt when
I have explained them they will be favorably received. The quantity
and the quality of the country that we, should we agree on the terms,
are about to relinquish our claim to has already been described. It is
a valuable district of rich lands and lies in a position very suitable
just now for the people of the State of Mississippi to own. All that,
I believe, is well understood by both parties. We, the red people, in
our private council last night, took into consideration and discussed
the subject as to the amount of inconvenience we shall suffer on this
side, and compared it with what may be termed advantages on the
other side of the Mississippi. We did it as fairly as we could, and I
am instructed to name the terms before the commissioners in council
to-day upon which we feel willing to swap countries. In the first
place, we shall, in addition to what had been already named and
agreed to, as one thing, claim that the United States must furnish
those who choose to go west with a good rifle gun, bullet molds, a
camp kettle, one blanket, and ammunition to last one year, corn to
support them on the journey and one year after getting there. The
United States must also send a good man for an agent, a good blacksmith, and furnish a trading house with Indian goods.

"We shall claim in the next place that the United States appoint
a good man, to be paid by the United States, whose duty it shall be
to use all reasonable exertions to collect the straggling Chahtas and
settle them upon the territory west of the Mississippi defined in this
treaty.

"In the next place, we claim that out of the lands we are about
to swap the United States for, fifty-four sections of a mile square
each shall be surveyed and sold to the best bidder by the United
States, for the purpose of raising a fund to support the Chahta
schools in the western country of the Chahtas, the whole to be

placed in the hands of the President of the United States to be dealt out by him for school purposes only in the Chahta nations.

"A good many of our people are dissatisfied with the manner, at the suggestion of the missionaries, in which $6,000 of their annuity has been taken from them by some of the chiefs. I claim that an additional tract of good land, in the country we are about to swap away, be set apart for raising a sum equal to that given away by the chiefs, so that the whole of the annuity may remain in the nation and be divided among them.

"One more specification and I am done. There are a good many warriors who have not been compensated for their services during the campaign to Pensacola. Pay them, and settle with those who have good houses and are living on the ceded territory, and if you, the commissioners, agree to what I have proposed, it is a bargain."

To all of these propositions the commissioners very readily assented, made satisfactory arrangements with those who resided on the ceded district, added to what Apushimataha had enumerated several other advantageous stipulations to the Chahtas in regard to their poor, and a few articles to please the missionaries, and the treaty was concluded.

The United States Commissioners first signed, then the three chiefs, after which one hundred leaders and warriors signed it. All were pleased and satisfied.

After the treaty was concluded and signed up, Apushimataha asked the privilege of making a few remarks, before the final breakup of the council, to his white friends and those of his own people who felt disposed to listen to him.

The two commissioners said they would take pleasure in hearing him. All the white people present said they should be delighted at it, and that they would wait with the greatest pleasure.

The Chahta moderators, numbering about twenty steady old men, who had handed pipes and preserved order during the whole time of the council, called the confused assembly to order again, handed round the pipes, at the close of which Apushimataha, after scanning his audience and laying his right hand on his left breast, said:

My heart throbs with feelings of deepest emotion while in the hearing of my own nation I make in their name to the two distinguished commissioners, General Jackson and General Hinds, and the great number of American people present, the declaration that we feel proud in the acknowledgment of the friendship and protecting care of their great nation, and that pride was increased almost to ecstacy when we heard it read as the last article in the treaty stipulations that that friendship should be perpetual. To me and to my feelings that article is more highly valued than all the balance of the treaty. In the midst of this large assemblage, this ocean of pleasant faces, brilliant eyes, all turned upon me whilst I say it, and the glorious, shining, cloudless sun that rules this bright day, ominous of good, I most solemnly declare that on my part the sacred words 'perpetual friendship' included in the last article of the treaty shall never be violated or suffer the slightest infringement. We have made many treaties with the United States, all conducted in peace and amicably carried out; but this last one, the greatest of all, has been peculiar in its stipulations, giving another and a stronger proof of the fostering care and protecting intentions of the United States towards their Chahta friends. In all our treaties we have been encouraged by them to institute schools, seminaries of learning, urging us to prepare ourselves as fast as possible to become citizens and members of that great nation. In the treaty which has been concluded to-day the subject of schools has been more particularly urged and appropriations more extensively provided than in any former treaty. The applauding murmur on that subject has passed through the camps of the red people. It meets their approbation. They will most certainly succeed. It is a peculiar trait of the Chahta character that all national movements turn out to be successes. I am pleased to hear so many speaking favorably of the school institutions. It tells me that they will have them. It is a national sentiment; and I here venture the prediction, for I am considered a sort of prophet anyhow, that the day will come, and there are many children and some grown men here to-day who will live to see it, when the highly improved Chahta shall hold office in the councils of the great nation of white people and in their wars with the nations of the earth. Mixed up in the armies of the white man, the fierce war whoop of the Chahta warrior shall strike terror and melt the hearts of an invading foe. Mind that. Apushimataha has this day declared it, and his words of prophecy are not uttered foolishly or trivially. I believe it thoroughly, and the contemplation of the great and so happy a change in condition of my people is cheering to this old heart.

To my good friends, the commissioners, I may be permitted to say that they have presided over and conducted the treaty with patience, prudence, justice, and great ability, and to the sober and exceedingly well behaved white men, spectators of the council, I acknowledge my unfeigned gratitude, and long hence, when far away in my wild forest home, my unerring memory will convey me back to this treaty ground, when, in imagination, I shall greet with deepest feelings of fraternal affection every white man that my good fortune has brought me in contract with while the treaty was in progress.

Individually, of my greatest and best friend, General Jackson, I shall not speak. My words would fail to express the deep sentiments of respect and fraternal affection I entertain for him. He is my good friend. That must suffice for this time.

To the chiefs, leaders and warriors of my own countrymen, I may say, return to your homes and forget not the words of this great treaty, to which so many of you subscribed your names with your white brothers to the same big paper this bright day. 'Nuktanla bilia' (perpetual peace) is placed on that paper. You have all agreed to it and manifested your consent by having your names placed on the big paper, where they will remain long after you have all passed away to the good hunting ground. Those names cannot now die, and so long as you live let it not be said that you have deviated in the slightest degree from what you have declared and accepted this day.

And now, with the strongest desire for the health and prosperity of this great multitude, with the very best feelings towards them, I pronounce that they are, with my hearty thanks, dismissed.

Apushimataha was at many councils and small arrangements with white people about St. Stephens and the United States trading houses, which was superintended by George S. Gaines. Being opposed to the missionaries, he made many brilliant speeches and arguments at the councils got up by them for the purpose of enriching themselves at the expense of the nation. Apukshinubi supported the missionary cause, submitting to their unrighteous claims on the people and their many false representations knowingly, for the sake of the small amount of hush money he received from them.

But Apushimataha understood their tricks, and he would not keep secret for them. He warned the Chahtas against their machinations and did what he could to enlighten his people on the subject. The Chahta people, however, being extremely superstitious, and being greatly frightened at the idea of the *haiyip hitul lakna* (yellow powder lake), many of them were too cowardly to listen to the warning voice of their great chief.

There was a yankee once who visited the Chahta people in search of material to compose a book, and being about the missionary establishments—the missionaries were also yankees—the book man attended one Chahta council, when he heard Apushimataha make one of his flaming speeches. He was so much pleased with the chief and his oratorical ability that he made up his mind to procure the necessary facts and write a history of the great man. He inquired of the missionaries as to his origin and early life. The missionaries knew nothing about it, of course, but they promised the book man that they would procure the information he required the very next day. They told him that Apushimataha was to make another one of his fine speeches the next day and they would prepare another speaking Indian who was friendly to the missionary cause to flatter the old chief a little as soon as he had finished his business speech, and as the old sinner could not resist flattery they would be certain to get the history of his origin. It is true, they said, that his origin is not known to any one alive, and he professed to be proud of the secret, but as we hold the key that will unlock the mystery we will work it out of him to-morrow.

To-morrow came, and after several speeches had been delivered, Apushimataha took the stand and continued to speak at least an hour. He was unusually eloquent, his arguments irresistible and his embellishment unique and unsurpassingly beautiful. The book man said that he had never before heard a speech from any man that would compare with it.

As soon as Apushimataha had taken his seat the chief that had been prepared by the missionaries for the purpose arose, and after a few flattering remarks on the subject of the masterly speech he had just heard, furthermore said that the history of the origin of so great a man should no longer be withheld from his own nation at least. He pressed it upon the chief as a right which his people could in justice claim of him, and he asked it of him in all kindness and in the name of the nation that he avail himself of the present occasion to rise up and at once relieve the minds of his people on that interesting topic.

Apushimataha immediately responded to this polite request by rising from his seat and taking the speaker's stand. After some few preliminary remarks on the subject of the vanity of aspirants to fame and political egotism, he very gravely delivered himself of the following wonderful account of his origin:

It was a long time ago; at the season when the glorious sun was pouring down his brightest, balmiest and greatest life-giving influence; when the gay flowers, bedecked in their most gorgeous habiliments, were sweetest, brightest and most numerous; when the joyous birds in full chorus were chanting their gleeful songs of life and love, full of inspiration; when all nature seemed to quiver in rapturous emotion. 'Twas noon. The day was calm and fair and very pleasant. There was a beautiful wide spreading plain, with but few trees on it. One there was of giant size and venerable age. It was a red oak, and its dark waving branches, overshadowing an immense area of the beautiful green plain, had bid defiance and braved unscathed the storms of many winters. There is stood, vast in it proportions, calm in its strength, majestic in its attitude. It had witnessed the rise and fall of many generations of animal life. But everything must have its time, fulfill its destiny. That magnificent red oak, the prominent feature on that far reaching landscape, and had been for centuries, had not accomplished the object for which the great spirit had planted it. There it was in full foliage, casting its dark, widely spreading shadow upon the sunlit plain. All nature was clad in smiles of joy on that bright day. Anon a cloud was rising in the west, a black, angry, threatening cloud, looming upwards and rapidly widening its scowling front. Harshly grumbling as it whirled its black folds onward, nearer and nearer, very soon it overspread the whole heavens, veiling the landscape in utter darkness and appalling uproar. It was a sweeping tornado, fringed with forked lightning, thunders rolling and bellowing; the winds fiercely howled and the solid earth trembled. In the height of this confusion and war of elements a burning flash of fire gleamed through the black obscurity. A shattering crash, followed by a burst of terrific thunder that, heavily rumbling through the surging storm, seemed to shake down the humid contents of the fast rolling cloud in irresistible torrents. Awful sounds assailed the startled senses in all directions as the frightful tornado swiftly swept by in its devastating course. Soon it passed and was all calm again. The sun poured down his beaming rays in their wonted brilliancy; but the vast, time honored sylvan king, the red oak, had been shivered into fragments; its oddshapen splinters lay widely scattered on the rain-beaten plain. Not a vestige remained to mark the spot where once stood that towering tree. Not even a snag of the stump remained. The object of its creation was accomplished, and in its place there was a new thing under the sun! Shall I name it? Equipped and ready for battle, holding in his right hand a ponderous club, standing erect on the place of the demolished red oak, was your dauntless chief, "Apushimataha."

He took his seat without making any further remarks. The missionaries were astounded when they found that the sagacious chief had scented out their secret design and played them off with so much integrity.[2] The book man said his speeches surpassed anything he had ever heard before, and that it was not only a great pity but it was a damaging loss to the literary world that no one had taken the pains to preserve them. He regretted very much that he was not prepared for it, that he might have preserved the speeches he had heard him deliver at the present council. He had heard them; they were wonderful, and that was about all he should be able to say on the subject.

Apushimataha attended only one more treaty. That treaty was held at Washington City, during which time he died of the croup. His speeches on that occasion were not preserved. On his deathbed he made a speech and it was published, but it has been mislaid or lost and will not appear in this little sketch of his history.

General Jackson and many other United States officers were gathered about the bedside of the dying chief. General Jackson bent over the prostrate form and inquired, "What is the last request of the chief?" "Bury me with the big guns firing over the grave," was the reply.

He was buried at Washington and an artillery salute fired over the grave as requested by the dying warrior. He was buried with all the honors of a brigadier general.

During the year 1812 Tecumsi sent his prophet on a visit to all the southern tribes. He passed through the Chahta nation, called a meeting at several places, where he made speeches and prophesied against the American people, predicting the downfall of the government of the United States, the utter destruction of the white people and there repossession of the whole continent by the red people. He told them also that he was then on his way to the Muskogee nation, that they would join in the great scheme of destroying the white people, and that any tribe of Indians who refused to aid in the restoration of the country would be looked upon as enemies and would be destroyed with the white people. The Great Spirit had said it, and it would be so.

The prophet made his first speech in Mushulatubbee's district at the house of Wm. Sternes, who was the public blacksmith. He confused the minds of the people considerably. So much so that John Pitchlynn, United States interpreter, to counteract the demoralizing influence of the prophesies, took the Bible, and reading it at a great many of their towns, showed the wavering people that there would never by any more prophets except false prophets, and the Big Book warned the people against them. They were compared to the blind leading the blind and would all go to ruin together.

The prophet went from the public smithy to the six towns, where he essayed to prophesy for them. He was there met by Apushimataha, who told him that he was a hireling, that his predictions were false, and that he must absent himself from the Chahta country. The prophet took Apushimataha at his word and passed immediately on to the Muskogee country. His prophecies had, however, been favorably received by some of the Chahtas, and forty-five families of them sent over and fought with the Muskogees against the whites. Apushimataha, with a brigade of Chahtas, joined the United States army and was of much assistance to them in the Creek war. As soon as the war had ended Apushimataha hunted up and put to the sword all he could of his traitor countrymen. Most of them, however, escaped, running into the marshy country below Mobile, Ala., where they remain to this day.

Soon after the death of Apushimataha I was down at Mobile

where I met with the leader of the fugitive Chahtas. I told them of the death of the old warrior chief and that they might go home now without any danger. He professed to be very proud of the opportunity to return in peace to his people, and early the next day I saw him coming into the city in front of the whole clan. They were marching in double files, the men in front and the women filling up the rear. There were nearly a hundred of them, and they were clean washed and well dressed in the Chahta costume. When I came near the leader he spoke to me, saying that his people were all greatly rejoiced at the prospect of returning to their country again, and, as they had no means to travel on, he had conceived of dressing the party in the best they had and make his women and warriors sing through all the streets that day, tell the people that they were going home if he could procure means to buy bread for his women and children on the journey. He said he could talk pretty good English and that he would go from door to door through the whole city and beg the people to give something to aid them on their journey. I told him that it was a good plan and to start the business I would give twenty-five cents. He took it and put it into an empty shot sack which he had in his hand, and the crowd that had gathered around to hear a while man talk Indian, when they found out what was going on all threw in something to the amount of perhaps five or six dollars. They commenced singing and passed on down the streets, telling their story in song, and the leader interpreting the song in as good English as he could, holding the sack to every one he met. They sang and walked the street all the day. I saw them when it was nearly night; he held up his sack showing me that it was nearly full. The next day I saw all the men, leader and all, in town drunk. The leader said to me that he made more money yesterday than he could have made in the Chahta country in a lifetime, and laughed heartily. He said also that his people were all rich and doing well. The women carried fat pine and sold it in town every day and the men hunted and sold a good deal of venison and a great many ducks and fish at good prices, and that they were rich, better off for clothes and provisions than any of the Chahtas in the nation. Upon being asked whose land they lived on he said he could not tell me, but he said:

It does not matter who the swamp belongs to. No one lives on it, nor does any white man ever go into it. It is all marsh or water, except an occasional dry spot of elevated ground. On these little islands we have our houses and live very comfortably and out of the way of the rest of the world. We have our canoes, and fish and hunt for ducks and other water fowls during the winter, and in the summer we move out of the marshy country into the pine woods lying between here and New Orleans. There it is dry and healthy and game is very plentiful. We shall never go back to the Chahta people again.

They are there yet, 1861.

Apushimataha, when in good society among the white people, deported himself very respectfully, and when he had a good interpreter to talk for him could make himself agreeably interesting.

During the first year of my residence in the Chahta country I finished a large and very excellent building. When it was completed the white people solicited me, for the novelty of having it in the Chahta nation, to give them a ball in the new house. I did so, and invited all three of the chiefs, the old national interpreter, John Pitchlynn, and a good many of the head men. The party was a very full one, well conducted, and it passed off in good style. Notwithstanding that they were often invited, none of the Chahtas, except a few educated half breeds, participated in the dance. They kept their seats, behaving very orderly, and were doubtless highly amused and deeply interested. To them it was a great performance, or a show, the like of which they had never before witnessed.

Apushimataha, after supper was over, desiring to render himself agreeable and to attract attention, as I then supposed, came to me and asked me to talk a little for him. The party being large, I had a good deal to attend to, and the national interpreter, who was a very lively man, being present, I went to him and got him to go and interpret for the chief. Apushimataha, pointing to a group of very finely dressed young ladies, told Pitchlynn, the interpreter, that he desired to have a little talk with them. Pitchlynn agreeing, they approached the group of young ladies and the chief said:

My friend, the interpreter, has often read in my presence from a big book which has many strange things. Amongst the rest of the very strange account was one about angels. The book said they looked exactly like people, and yet they were so delicate in their formation that the inhabitants of this world could not feel them when they tried to handle them. Now, I have been observing these six bright and most elegantly beautiful beings all night, and I have come to the conclusion that if there are any such beings as angels, a thing I never before credited, these must be some of them. To satisfy my great curiosity on the subject, I solicited my friend to come and talk for me, and to ask the privilege for me to touch the pretty creatures to see if I could feel them.

Pitchlynn told them what he said, and they being greatly flattered readily consented that the chief might satisfy his curiosity by feeling of them. Apushimataha then proceeded in a most delicate and polite manner possible, using only his thumb and middle finger, to grasp very gently the arm of one of them. After touching them in several places until his hand was nearly at the shoulder, he turned to Pitchlynn and said: "It's folks, for I can feel it very distinctly, but without the experiment I should never have believed. It is sure enough somebody, and I must say a mighty nice somebody. But perhaps they are not all people; some of them may yet turn out to be *uba hatak* (angels); I must touch all of them before I can be satisfied about it."

And so he paid them the compliment of taking hold of the arm of each of the six young ladies. When he had got through with it he told the interpreter to say to them that he had convinced himself that they were people, inhabitants of earth, a conclusion he should never have been able to come to except by the experiment of actual contact. Pitchlynn delivered his speech to the young ladies and they acknowledged that they felt themselves highly complimented.

With all his good qualities and his extraordinary abilities, Apushimataha was an incorrigible drunkard. He would not touch liquor when any business was on hand. It was only when he was idle that he indulged in drinking. He was quite poor, and did not seem to care for property enough to strive for its accumulation. He made but few debts, and was always very prompt in discharging them at the time of their becoming due.

The few items of history which I have preserved are, as far as I know, all that is now certainly known of that truly great man. I consider it not only a pity but a great wonder that some of those gentlemen about Gainesville (trading house) who were so long and so familiarly acquainted with him did not think of preserving an account of his history. They could all tell many wonderful stories of the actions and public speeches of Apushimataha. Yet they never attempted to place any of it on paper that I ever heard of.

Nitakgachi succeeded Apushimataha and was a very good chief. He was good looking, fine formed, medium sized, a very fluent speaker, and was quite popular both in his own country and among the white people. I never saw him but once and that was at a large collection of Indians at the Yahnubi old fields. The council was called to consider the propriety of driving the missionaries out of the nation. They had erected a bush arbor that shaded a quarter of an acre of ground. In the center of the arbor was a square vacancy, that admitted the rays of the sun through it to the ground, which illuminated a spot about twelve feet in diameter. Through this vacancy went up a very tall pole upon the top of which floated to the breeze the American flag. I know not where they had procured this flag or who it was that had suggested the idea of the liberty pole. It was there when I arrived. In the sunshine that fell through the hole in the arbor was where those who desired to address the people had to stand while speaking. This had been a custom with the Chahtas from time immemorial. The object was to prevent them from speaking too long.

The audience were all seated in the shade, while the speaker stood in the sunshine. They said they could bear to be comfortably seated in the shade as long as the orator could stand and speak in the hot sunshine.

The day I allude to on Yahnubi was a very hot summer day, and they made about eighty speeches. Of course they were short ones. They had declared independence of the missionary party of Chahtas, which had grown to be quite large and troublesome, and with a few exceptions the speeches that were made that day were simply public declarations of their sentiments in relation to the missionaries.

They had commenced speaking early and by the middle of the day a number of them had already expressed their sentiments on the subject. It was summer time and just about twelve o'clock, when the rays of the meridian sun were falling perpendicularly through the aperture in the arbor, Nitakgachi stepped into the bright spot. He was dressed in full regimentals, laces, buttons, epaulettes, bright and sparkling in the sunshine, had a fine effect, and the murmur of admiration arose universally from the seated multitude. He cast his eyes around upon his extensive audience, and was in the act of commencing his speech when a little flow of wind whirled the flag around, casting its shadow upon him. He very deliberately turned up his face, and fixing his eyes, gazed on the flag for nearly a minute. Then, turning to his audience, he exclaimed:

> I feel proud that the shadow of the flag falls upon me this clear day—that beautiful ensign of the truly great nation. I have been informed by men who know that the shadow of that flag falls upon every land under the sun, and that it is a free pass, and is hailed with respect by all the nations of the earth. It is looked upon as the ensign of liberty by all peoples; and as a token of respect to the wonderful nation whose flag it is, we, too, have adopted it as the ensign of liberty and independence which we shall declare and make known this auspicious day. I look upon the blue sky; it is clear; not a speck of cloud is seen in any direction. The bright sun pours down his flashing rays unobstructed, save by the waving folds of the great nation's flag, and I am enveloped in its shadow. I take it for a good omen; therefore I feel proud. The Great Spirit has swept the vaulted sky of every speck of cloud; he has made the sun brighter than ordinary on this occasion, and he has sent a little breath of wind to throw the shadow of that great symbol of liberty upon me to assure me of his approbation of the principle I am about to declare. Therefore I repeat it, that I am proud that the shadow of the flag of liberty falls upon me this day.

He then went on speaking on the subject that had been the cause of the meeting.

Nitakgachi went with his people when they were removed west of the Mississippi, and that ends my knowledge of him.

There were several other fine speakers at Yanubi old fields that day, and some of them so nearly imitated Apushimataha in their gestures and the sound of their voices that I was forcibly struck with them, and on making inquiries in relation to who they were, I was told that Apushimataha, during his lifetime, kept a regular school of oratory and that these fine speakers were some of his students. A thing I was not before apprised of.

Mashulatubbee's mouthpiece, Aiahokatubi, was a fluent speaker and a close, cogent, reasoning orator. He was of the philosophic turn of mind, and seemed to enjoy himself best when alone. He was seldom seen except at their councils, and then was rarely heard to say anything. He spoke only when he was called upon by his chief, and then everybody crowded up to hear him. His attitude, gesticulation, the musical tones of his voice and his great reasoning powers placed him in my estimation as an orator second only to Apushimataha. He was an unbeliever in the missionary dogmas, and as he would on all public occasions express boldly his irreligious science, he gave the missionaries considerable trouble.

There were many more quite conspicuous and very good men in the Chahta nation at the time I resided there, whose history would be interesting to any inquiring mind. All of which, however, is forever lost. I remember the names of only a few of them. There was General Hlikooohlo (humming bird), Captain Nashobanowa (walking wolf), Peachlichiiskitina (little leader), and many more whose names would not now interest the reader.

They were all warriors, a title none could bear until he had killed somebody in battle, then the war name that is bestowed by the *Ishlahullo* only tells how the killing was performed. As Piantubbi (hallo and kill it), Hablautibi (kick and kill), Filematubi (turn back and kill), etc., ubi is to kill, and nearly all war names end with ubi.

Notes

1. "The Autobiography of Gideon Lincecum" will be found in Volume VIII of the *Publications of the Mississippi Historical Society*, pp. 443–519. This contribution is particularly valuable because of the insight which it gives into pioneer life. The same volume also contains another contribution from the pen

of Dr. Lincecum entitled "Choctaw Traditions; about Their Settlement in Mississippi and the Origin of Their Mounds." Through the kindness of his daughter, Mrs. S. L. Doren, of Hempstead, Texas, this further contribution from Dr. Lincecum is published for the first time. As is shown by internal evidence his "Life of Apushimataha" was written in the year 1861. Since that time the manuscript has been carefully preserved and is now in well-nigh perfect condition.

The editor of these publications takes pleasure in reproducing in this connection a brief newspaper sketch by Dr. Lincecum, which was published in *The Galveston and Dallas News* several years ago, the exact date being now unknown. This sketch is as follows:

I have always regretted that when the opportunity did exist I had not made myself more familiar with the habits, manners, customs and traditions of the Choctaw Indians, who, at the time of my birth, owned and occupied more than half of the lands in the territory of Mississippi. From my earliest recollection down to 1837–8, when they were removed by the Government to lands set apart for them in what is known as the Reservation, I was brought into intimate relations with them, and contracted a friendship for many individuals which long survived their exodus. They were firm in their attachments, strong in their prejudices and slow to forget or forgive an injury. They would not voluntarily submit to any restraint which would deprive them of entire freedom of action. And this sentiment pervaded all ages and conditions of life. The Indian, during several months in the year, made the forest his home, and here, protected by barks, usually taken from the gum and poplar, he dressed the skin of the deer killed in the chase, extracted oil from the fat of the bear, and prepared choice portions of the bear and the deer, either for market or to supply his family with food.

Their knowledge of the stars and of woodcraft was developed to an extraordinary degree, and if they made no progress in the arts and the sciences, they could travel for hundreds of miles with unerring precision, having no other guide than the sun and the starts or some peculiarity in the appearance of the trees, as they faced the north or the south. Many of them understood our language, but they spoke it rarely, and not then from choice. On returning from a hunting excursion, they were fond of relating their adventures; the perils they had encountered and the number of bear and deer they had killed. No interruption occurred, nor was any question asked during the recital, but when the speaker came to a pause and sufficient time had been given for the collection of such little fragments as had been overlooked or forgotten in the recital, then, and not till then, did the conversation become general. They were good talkers and patient listeners, and in this latter trait they might have been imitated with advantage by those who affected a higher order of intellectual culture. But they are fast passing away under the mismanagement of the Government, which has too frequently employed as its agents men who looked more to their own interests than they did to the wards of the nation.

Like the white man the Indian had his superstitions, but he had no written history. Some of his traditions carry us back to ancient Greece, if not the cradle the school of that mythology whose influence is still observable, not only among the heathen, but in the habits and literature of the most enlightened nations. We all know that the gods of the ancients were as numerous as the stars which shine above us, and that in the van of them stood Jupiter Olympus, who, for a god, assumed many strange and, we might add, very undignified characters, and was subject to all the passions and many of the infirmities of humanity. He deserves to be immortal. But for him Troy would not have been destroyed; Achilles would have had no cause of quarrel with Agamemnon; Homer would not have written the Iliad, nor Virgil the Aeneid, and the fame of Pope and Dryden would have been partially eclipsed as translators.

Jupiter was a god of power and gave birth, in a very extraordinary manner, to the impersonation of the highest order of intellect. With a blow of his brazen hatchet, Vulcan cleft the head of Jupiter and Minerva leaped forth in panoply. This is a beautiful allegory, but it is not as grand in its conception as that of the birth of Pushmataha (Son of Thunder), who had neither father nor mother, but directed by the Great Spirit a thunderbolt struck a giant oak, and Pushmataha leaped forth, a young warrior, armed and painted, to go on the warpath. To this day many of the Choctaws adhere to this legend, and though he died in 1824 they still believe that he was only called away by the Great Spirit for consultation, and that when plans for the future prosperity of their country are fully matured he will return and again teach them the arts of peace, or, if necessary, lead them successfully against their enemies.

During the Creek war of 1813-14, Pushmataha . . . joined General Jackson with a large number of his warriors and fought with distinction in all the battles of that eventful period—Talladega, Holy Ground and Pensacola—and accompanied General Jackson to New Orleans, where, without being a participant, he witnessed the battle of January 8, 1815. He was a proud man and, holding the commission of colonel from the Government, looked down with sovereign contempt on those of a lower grade. When asked by Captain Jack to join him in a drink he treated the invitation as an insult to his dignity, but immediately afterwards drank with General Claiborne, in whom he recognized a peer.

In 1824 Pushmataha and several other chiefs went to Washington to see the President, and, if possible, to obtain a settlement of the debt due by the Government, originating in the treaty held at Doak's Stand in 1820, and known as the "Net proceeds claim." After three of the chiefs had died the others returned home, without accomplishing anything. Strange as it may appear, this debt was recognized and paid by the Government in 1888, amounting to more than $1,000,000. If this was a just claim in 1888 it must have been equally so in 1824. I cannot imagine any cause of this long delay of about sixty-five years. And yet, in the face of these acts of bad faith or wanton neglect, people pretend to be astonished that there should be an occasional manifestation of hostility on the part of the Indians. The injuries inflicted on them have frequently been of the most aggravating character, and if now and then they become restive under insult and oppression it should not be a matter of surprise.

While in Washington Pushmataha was frequently the guest of the President and other Government officials. He had also the pleasure of meeting Lafayette, to whom he made a brief but very eloquent address, the closing paragraph shadowing forth a prophecy which was fulfilled before the close of the year, being: "We heard your name in our distant wigwams. I longed to see one who had come a long way to assist our friends of the white race when they were a small people. I have seen and shaken you by the hand. This is our last meeting on earth. Soon the great ocean will divide us. We shall see each other no more till we meet in the happy hunting ground."

Big dinners and champagne were too much for a constitution that had imbibed so freely of whisky, not always of the best quality. He could digest 'possum and rabbit on the waters of Bucatunna, the place where weaving is done, but the highly seasoned dishes served at the Presidential mansion brought on a complication of diseases that resulted in his death on the night of the 23d of December, 1824. A niece of David Folsom, one of the chiefs who accompanied the delegation to Washington, in the character of "interpreter and treasurer," sent me a copy of a letter written by her uncle on the 24th and 25th of December, 1824, giving a highly interesting narrative of the last sickness, death and burial of Pushmataha, from which I shall make some extracts.

"I take up my pen to inform you that Chief Pushmataha is no more. He died last night, about 12 o'clock. He has complained ever since he came here with sore throat. But when he indulged moderately in strong drink he felt better. But his drink was great. He was always worse after the big dinners he attended. I finally concluded that he would never return home. But he continued to expose himself, until finally, about 9 o'clock on the morning of the 23d, he fell on the street and was conveyed to his room, where he was attended by two physicians, but without effect. Many friends and strangers called to see him, among others General Jackson, to whom his last words were addressed: 'When I am dead let the big guns be fired over me.'

"We were at a loss how to proceed with his burial, but the Government took charge of it. He was buried with the honors of war. Several military companies turned out, as well as the marines from the navy yard and two bands of music. It was a great procession. We took the body of our departed chief in the presence of several thousand people. We marched in company of and in the way of those people to the burial ground. He was laid in the grave. The minister prayed for us. When it was over he was covered with cold clay, and we left him in the midst of many hundred people. I assure you, my dear friend, I am thankful there was so much honor paid to our departed chief. Many Congressmen, as well as General Jackson, treated us with great kindness. I can truly say that we have received every mark of friendship and brotherly love from the white people since we have been among them. We are still here doing nothing; that is, we have as yet done nothing, nor do I think there is any chance for succeeding in the business that brought us to this city. I regret to say that I cannot be useful to the delegation, because they will have their own way, and will not have an ear for such a poor person as I am. While I act very independently before them, I treat them with affectionate kindness. It will be a wonder to me if all the delegates return home. Pushmataha was conscious up to the moment of dissolution, and occasionally conversed with the friends in attendance. As you go home you will see beautiful flowers and hear the birds singing in the trees—but Pushmataha will see and hear them no more. When you go to our people they will ask, where is Pushmataha? And you will answer, 'He is no more.' They will hear it as the fall of a mighty oak of a still day in the midst of the forest."

Many years ago I visited the congressional burying ground to pay my respects to the greatest chief of the Choctaw Nation. A modest monument, erected by the chiefs, marks his resting place, on which is inscribed his last words: "When I am dead let the big guns be fired over me." If, as Paul says, "They that have not the law are a law unto themselves," then will the heaven of the Indian be as bright and beautiful as the paradise of Mahommet and none will enter therein more worthy of Divine favor than Pushmataha.

Regardless of the legends, the Pushmataha of history was born in 1764, on the east bank of the Noxubee River, two miles above Macon, on what was known in after years as the Howard plantation. Near the place of his birth there stood, and may stand at this day, a large black oak, which was held in reverence by his people as marking the place of his birth. The little log cabin in which he first saw the light has long since disappeared, but the traditional location has been faithfully preserved by the Indians who now inhabit that part of Mississippi. It is their Mecca. Like many other great men, he acquired no distinction from his birth, and would have said with Iphicrates, "I am not only the son of my own actions, but the first of my family that achieved anything worthy of finding a place in history." He was not the only great man that could make this arrogant boast, and yet he was greater than many who have realized fame and fortune, by means more equivocal than any that marked his career.

He early distinguished himself both as a hunter and warrior, and at an early age, when few aspired to the dignity, was appointed one of the principal chiefs, which position he maintained till his death, in 1824. He was always the friend of the white man, and when Tecumseh visited the south in 1811, with a view to uniting the Indians north and south against our people, he indignantly spurned the proposition, telling him that while temporary success might be obtained at one point, disasters that would more than counterbalance them would be experienced in other quarters. Besides, the Creeks, who joined the league, were his hereditary enemies. While he was very young the Creeks made an unexpected raid among the Choctaws, during which his father and mother were killed. At a subsequent period, when he had acquired fame as a warrior, a party of Creeks who were on a marauding expedition plundered his house and then set it on fire. This was an indignity which a Choctaw chief could not submit to. He immediately called together thirty of his young men, followed the marauders, overtook and killed the entire party. Not satisfied with this summary punishment, he made a raid into the country of the Creeks and brought away much booty and many scalps. His subsequent career forms part of the history of the south. He held the commission of colonel in the United States Army and served with distinction down to the capture of Pensacola, though he was not discharged from service until January 27, 1815. I have a report from the War Department to that effect.

Though distinguished as a warrior, he gained, if possible, higher honors as a statesman, orator and diplomatist. In all the treaties entered into with the United States he was the leader, and showed, by his consummate skill, that he was worthy the confidence of his people. One of my correspondents in the Indian Territory says that in "eloquence he was the peer of Daniel Webster." This may be just praise, as he had been a student of nature, and from her vast storehouse enriched his discourses by drawing liberally and with an artist's imagination those beautiful images with which all his speeches, and even his ordinary conversation, so frequently abounded. When the United States asked the privilege of opening a road from Nashville to Natchez for the transportation of the mails and for ordinary travel, the privilege was unhesitatingly granted, but it was coupled with the condition that all the public houses, way stations and ferries should be held by the Indians. No white man could trade among them without having first obtained a license, for which he had to pay a stipulated sum. This was one of Pushmataha's favorite measures.

But with all his excellent qualities there mingled some vices, which, being too freely indulged, carried him prematurely to the grave. He was an inveterate drunkard, a habit which he indulged to such an excess that it could only be repressed when business of importance claimed his attention. Accompanied by his friend Piamingo, one of the minor chiefs, they would go to Memphis, and taking up their quarters at Fort Pickering, then in charge of a few United States soldiers, they would sally out, and, in the language of an old resident of that place, for several days "paint the town red."

In July, 1823, he went to see the Indian agent, W. Ward, a distance of eighty miles. On the 4th Major Pitchlynn gave a dinner party, to which Pushmataha was invited, and as usual drank a good deal of whisky. In the evening, when he started home, Mr. Ward discovered that he had no horse, and suggested to the Major that one should be presented to him. The gift was made, coupled with the condition that he should not sell him for liquor. Some months later he again appeared at the agency, but on foot as usual. When reproached by the Major for violating his pledge he very naively replied: "Yes, I did promise you, in the presence of others, that I would not sell him for liquors, but I made no promise not to bet him off on a game of ball." He often staked all he possessed on a game of ball, sometimes without success, though he might have been a match for some of the best players at Audubon Park.

In reply to an inquiry one of my correspondents in the Indian Territory writes: "The great chief was of medium height, but portly. Much strong drink had bloated his face, but his eyes never lost their brilliancy. Even towards the close of life no one could listen to his speeches without being impressed with his eloquence. He had a fine command of language, a musical voice, and every gesture was appropriate to the subject." In his last interview with the President he had intended to make a long speech, giving his views of the relations between the two countries and mapping out the policy which each should respectively pursue, but he was too unwell to proceed. All he could say was: "I can say, and speak the truth, that neither I nor my father nor any of my ancestors ever drew bow in anger against the people of the United States. We have been true in our friendship; we have held your hand so long that our fingers, like the claw of an eagle, will not let them go. Another will address you; I am too, unwell to proceed." In less than forty-eight hours the great chief had entered the "happy hunting ground." Peace to his memory.

2. I did not attend many of their councils, consequently did not often hear Apushimataha speak; and of those I did hear, except the above and his speech at the table of the five magistrates in the Atoba case, my notes are all meager, only preserving the substances of his subjects, clothed in my language, which but poorly represents the original. His inimitable eloquence was the theme of conversation with many learned men, and strange as it may appear, no one that I ever heard of ever attempted to preserve any of his speeches or any facts in relation to his history.

INDEX

Aiahokatubi, 28, 96
Alocheway (Alachua) Indians, 74
Apuckshinubi, 26, 29, 38, 73, 86
Apushamatahahubi, see Pushmataha
Atoba, 31–33, 35–41, 102

ball game, see stickball

Chahta, see Choctaw
Chahta trading house, treaty
    of, 73
Chahta Immataha, xii–xiii
Chickasaws, xi, 21–23
Chickashas, see Chickasaws
Choctaws,
    ancestral remains, 1–2, 4–7, 9–12,
        14–16, 17, 25
    description, 97
    elections, 27
    "fugitives," 91–92
    history, xii–xiv
    knowledge, vii
    language, vii, x, 96
    medicine, 27
    population, 17
    schools, 83, 85, 96
    warfare, see entries for Ovashsashi
        and Muskogee/Creeks
Claiborne, General, 98
Cocke, William, 38–40
Coffee, John, 73
Comanche Indians, 80
corn, cultivation of, 3, 4, 16, 21
Creek nation, 100–101, see also
    Muskogees
Creek War of 1818, 74–75, 90

Darwin, Charles, vii
Dinsmore, Silas, 73
disease, in Mississippi, x

Doak's Stand treaty, xv, 74, 98
Doran, Sallie (Lincecum), vii

education, in Mississippi, ix
Eliccha Chito, x–xi, xiv

Federal road, viii
Folsom, David, 99
Fort Confederation, 72
    treaty of, xv, 73
Fort Mims, xv
Fulahooma, xii
Fulsome, Edmund, 74

Gaines, George S., 86
green corn dance (and feast), 4, 12–
    14, 16–17

Hinds, General, 74, 79, 82–83, 85
Hlikooohlo, General, 96

Iksas, Choctaw clans, 2, 5, 12, 26–27,
    58, 62
Indian Removal Act of 1830, xi
Indian Territory (Oklahoma), xiii
Isht Ahullo (ishlahullo), Choctaw
    spiritual official, 2, 6, 8, 17–18, 20,
    63, 96
Isi maleli, 3

Jack, Captain, 98
Jackson, Andrew, xiv, xv, 58, 74–77,
    79–82, 85–86, 89, 98–99

Lafayette, Marquis de, 99
Lincecum, Gideon, vii–ix
Lincecum, Hezekiah, viii
Lincecum, Sally Hickman, viii
Lincecum, Sarah, vii, 36
Lincecum family, vii–viii

Long Arrow, 7, 24
Lopina, 13

Mackey, Middleton, 74
McKee, John, 73–74
Mikisukies (Miccosukees), 74
military road, 28
Mingo Hamstubi, 73
missionaries, 84, 86–87, 89, 94, 96
Mushulatubi (Mushulatubbee,
  Mashulatubbee), 27–31, 36, 38,
  90, 96
Muskogees, 58–60, 63–64, 74, 78, 90

Nanih Waya (Nunih Waya) camp
  and mound, xiii, 3–4, 9, 13–14, 16,
  18, 21–24
  dimensions, 12, 25n. 2
Nashobanowa, Captain, 96
Nitakgachi, 94–95

Okla Falaya (western Choctaws), xiii
Okla Hannali (Six Towns Choc-
  taws), xiii, xiv, 90
Okla Tannap (eastern Choctaws), xiii
Ovashsashi (Osage) nation, 43–56,
  58, 64–72, 80

Parker, Luther "Louis," 30–31, 33
Peachlichiiskitina, 96
Peni ikbi, 17
Pensacola campaign, 84, 98
Philadelphia Academy of Science, vii
Piamingo, 101
Pitchlynn, John, viii–ix, xii, 34–35,
  41, 73–74, 90, 92–93, 101
Pitchlynn, John, Jr., ix
pole, liberty, 94
pole, sacred, 2, 4, 8, 12, 17, 20–22, 25

Pushapuknuk, treaty of, 73
Pushmataha, xiv–xvi, 26, 29–30, 38–
  41, 86–87, 92
  and alcohol, 93, 99, 101
  appearance, 101–102
  death of, 89, 99–100
  meaning of name, xv, 63–64
  origin, 88–89, 98, 100
  young manhood among Choc-
    taws, 41–72
  represents tribe in treaties, 73–85
  ally of United States, 74–75, 77–
    78, 90, 98, 100

Red Stick Creeks, xv
Rhea, John, 73
Robertson, James, 73

Shukhah-anumpula, xii
Smithsonian Institution, vii
Spaniards, 72
Sternes, William, 90
stickball, xii, 101
sun emblem, sacred, 13–14

Tecumsi (Tecumseh), 90, 100
Tombigbee river, viii
tool carriers, Choctaw functionaries,
  3, 7, 11–12, 18–19, 24
Trail of Tears, xiv
Tuscaloosa, battle of, 58–61
Tuscona Hopaia, 72–73

Ward, W., 101
Wilkinson, James, Brigadier General,
  72–73

yushpakammi "spirit talkers and conjurers," 7–8, 18–20